WORKBOOK

4
FOCUS
ON
GRAMMAR
AN INTEGRATED SKILLS APPROACH

THIRD EDITION

MARJORIE FUCHS

MARGARET BONNER

with JANE CURTIS

PEARSON
Longman

Focus on Grammar 4: An Integrated Skills Approach
Workbook

Pearson Education, 10 Bank Street, White Plains, NY 10606

Staff credits: The people who made up the **Focus on Grammar 4 Workbook** team, representing editorial, production, design, and manufacturing, are listed below: Rhea Banker, Aerin Csigay, Karen Davy, Christine Edmonds, Nancy Flaggman, Ann France, Diana George, Laura Le Dréan, and Kathleen Silloway.
Cover images: Large shell, background, Nick Koudis, RF; large shell, center image, Kaz Chiba; background, Comstock Images, RF
Text design: Quorum Creative Services, Rhea Banker
Text composition: ElectraGraphics, Inc.
Text font: 11/13 Sabon, 10/13 Myriad Roman
Illustrator: Steven Schulman, p. 137.
Text credits: **p. 65,** Francine Klagsbrun, *Married People: Staying Together in the Age of Divorce.* New York: Bantam Books, 1985; **p. 68,** Eva Hoffman, *Lost in Translation: A Life in a New Language.* New York: Penguin, 1989; Ben Fong-Torres, *The Rice Room.* New York: Hyperion, 1994; Erich Von Däniken, *Chariots of the Gods?* New York: G.P. Putnam, 1977; **p. 69,** Antoine de Saint-Exupéry, *The Little Prince.* New York: Harcourt Brace, 1943; Margaret Mead, *Male and Female.* New York: William Morrow, 1949; Jay Matthews, *Escalante: The Best Teacher in America.* New York: Henry Holt, 1988; p. 70, Jean M. Auel, *The Clan of the Cave Bear.* New York: Crown, 1980; **p. 84,** Michael D. Lemonick, "Secrets of the Maya," *Time,* August 9, 1993; **pp. 119 and 122,** Maxine P. Fisher, *Walt Disney.* New York: Franklin Watts, 1988; **p. 123,** *Bottom Line Personal,* June 15, 1993. From an interview with Bob Sehlinger, author of *The Unofficial Guide to Walt Disney World and EPCOT,* 1993 edition. New York: Prentice Hall Travel; **p. 125,** Lisa Davis, "A Doubtful Device," *Health,* October, 1992, **pp. 92–95.**
Photo credits: **p. 6** PictureQuest; **p. 16** Kimberly White/Reuters/Corbis; **p. 21** Bettmann/Corbis; **p. 39** Getty Images; **p. 50** JLP/Deimos/Corbis; **p. 56** Atta Kenare/Getty Images; **p. 60** Jon Feingersh/zefa/Corbis; **p. 75** AP/Wide World Photos; **p. 119** General Photographic Agency/Getty Images; **p. 121** Bettmann/Corbis; **p. 141** Paul J. Richards/Getty Images.

ISBN: 0-13-191235-6 (Workbook)

LONGMAN ON THE **WEB**

Longman.com offers online resources for teachers and students. Access our Companion Websites, our online catalog, and our local offices around the world.

Visit us at **longman.com.**

Printed in the United States of America
5 6 7 8 9 10—BAH—12 11 10 09 08 07

Contents

Part IX: Conditionals

Part X: Indirect Speech and Embedded Questions

About the Authors

Marjorie Fuchs has taught ESL at New York City Technical College and LaGuardia Community College of the City University of New York and EFL at the Sprach Studio Lingua Nova in Munich, Germany. She holds a master's degree in Applied English Linguistics and a Certificate in TESOL from the University of Wisconsin–Madison. She has authored and co-authored many widely used books and multimedia materials, notably **Crossroads**, **Top Twenty ESL Word Games: Beginning Vocabulary Development**, **Families: Ten Card Games for Language Learners**, **Focus on Grammar 3 and 4: An Integrated Skills Approach**, **Focus on Grammar 3 and 4 CD-ROM**, **Longman English Interactive 3 and 4**, **Grammar Express Basic**, **Grammar Express Basic CD-ROM**, **Grammar Express Intermediate**, and the workbooks to the **Longman Dictionary of American English**, the **Longman Photo Dictionary**, **The Oxford Picture Dictionary**, **Focus on Grammar 3**, and **Grammar Express Basic.**

Margaret Bonner has taught ESL at Hunter College and the Borough of Manhattan Community College of the City University of New York, at Taiwan National University in Taipei, and at Virginia Commonwealth University in Richmond. She holds a master's degree in Library Science from Columbia University; and she has done work toward a Ph.D. in English Literature at the Graduate Center of the City University of New York. She has authored and co-authored numerous ESL and EFL print and multimedia materials, including textbooks for the national school system of Oman, **Step into Writing: A Basic Writing Text**, **Focus on Grammar 3 and 4: An Integrated Skills Approach**, **Grammar Express Basic CD-ROM**, **Grammar Express Basic Workbook**, **Grammar Express Intermediate**, **Focus on Grammar 3 and 4 CD-ROM**, **Longman English Interactive 4**, and **The Oxford Picture Dictionary Intermediate Workbook.**

Jane Curtis began teaching ESOL in Spain, where she participated in a Fulbright exchange program between the University of Barcelona and the University of Illinois at Urbana-Champaign. She currently teaches at Roosevelt University in Chicago, Illinois. She holds a master's degree in Spanish from the University of Illinois at Urbana-Champaign and a master's degree in Applied Linguistics from Northeastern Illinois University.

Simple Present and Present Progressive

1 | SPELLING: SIMPLE PRESENT AND PRESENT PROGRESSIVE

Write the correct forms of the verbs.

Base Form	Simple Present Third-Person Singular	Present Participle
1. answer	*answers*	*answering*
2. _____	asks	_____
3. buy	_____	_____
4. _____	_____	coming
5. _____	does	_____
6. eat	_____	_____
7. _____	_____	employing
8. _____	_____	flying
9. forget	_____	_____
10. _____	has	_____
11. hurry	_____	_____
12. _____	_____	lying
13. open	_____	_____
14. rain	_____	_____
15. reach	_____	_____
16. _____	says	_____
17. tie	_____	_____
18. _____	_____	traveling

2 | SIMPLE PRESENT AND PRESENT PROGRESSIVE

Complete the conversations with the correct form of the verbs in parentheses—simple present or present progressive. Use contractions when possible.

A. AMBER: I _____*think*_____ I've seen you before. _____ you
   1.(think)

   _____ Professor Bertolucci's course this semester?
   2.(take)

NOËL: No, but my twin sister, Dominique, _____ Italian this year.
   3.(study)

AMBER: That _____ her! I _____ her name now. You two
   4.(be)   5.(remember)

   _____ exactly alike.
   6.(look)

B. JARED: _____ you _____ that woman over there?
   1.(know)

TARO: That's Mangena. She usually _____ a pronunciation class at the
   2.(teach)

   Institute, but she _____ in the computer lab this term.
   3.(work)

JARED: That's an interesting name. What _____ it _____?
   4.(mean)

TARO: I'm not sure. I _____ I've ever known anyone else with that name.
   5.(not believe)

C. ROSA: How _____ you _____ your name?
   1.(spell)

ZHUŌ: Here, I'll write it down for you.

ROSA: You _____ unusual handwriting. It _____ very artistic.
   2.(have)   3.(look)

D. IVY: Hi. Why _____ you _____ there with such a terrible look
   1.(sit)

   on your face? You _____ too happy.
   2.(not seem)

LEE: I _____ to read this letter from my friend. He _____
   3.(try)   4.(not like)

   to use a computer, so he _____ his letters by hand and his handwriting
   5.(write)

   _____ awful. It _____ to get on my nerves.
   6.(be)   7.(begin)

E. AMY: _____ you _____ to hear something interesting? Justin
   1.(want)

   _____ to become a graphologist.
   2.(study)

CHRIS: What exactly _____ a graphologist _____?
   3.(do)

AMY: A graphologist _____ people's handwriting. You can learn a lot about
   4.(analyze)

   people from the way they _____—especially from how they
   5.(write)

   _____ their name.
   6.(sign)

3 | SIMPLE PRESENT AND PRESENT PROGRESSIVE

Complete this article. Use the correct form of the verbs in parentheses—simple present or present progressive. Sometimes there is more than one correct answer.

Right now Pam O'Neil _____*is taking*_____ a test, but she _____ it. She
               1. (take)   **2. (not know)**

_____ on what she _____—not on how her handwriting
 3. (focus)   **4. (write)**

_____. The person who will analyze the test is a graphologist—someone
 5. (look)

who _____ handwriting. Graphologists _____ that a
     6. (study)   **7. (believe)**

person's handwriting _____ an indication of his or her personality and
                     8. (give)

character. These days, many businesses _____ graphologists to help them
                             9. (use)

decide who to hire.

What exactly _____ company graphologist Perry Vance _____
                                         10. (hope)

to learn from applicants' writing samples? "I always _____ for clues to possible
                              11. (look)

behavior," he explained. "For example, the slant of the writing usually _____ a
                                    12. (tell)

lot. _____ the writing _____ to the left or to the right? A left slant
                     13. (lean)

often _____ a shy personality. The position of the sample on the page is also
     14. (indicate)

important," Vance continued. "The right-hand margin of the page _____ the
                               15. (represent)

future. Here's a writing sample from an executive who right now _____ a new
                             16. (plan)

direction for a large company. Notice that this person _____ much room in the
                         17. (not leave)

right-hand margin. This is the writing of someone who never _____ looking at
                         18. (avoid)

the future."

"What about signatures?" I asked. "Yes, signatures _____ us a lot about
                         19. (show)

someone," said Vance. "Look at this one by a chief executive officer of a large firm. He

_____ in the news a lot these days because the government _____
 20. (be)   **21. (investigate)**

his company. Those very large strokes are typical of a person who _____ about
                            22. (think)

himself first and _____ advantage of other people." Vance always
          23. (take)

_____, however, that his analysis _____ an applicant's future job
 24. (warn)   **25. (not guarantee)**

performance. There's no substitute for careful review of a complete application.

4 | EDITING

Read this e-mail from a student to her favorite English teacher. There are ten mistakes in the use of the simple present and the present progressive. The first mistake is already corrected. Find and correct nine more.

Hi!

    Well, I'm here at my new school, and ~~I'm liking~~ *I like* it very much. I'm study English this semester, but the classes are really different from our English classes in Korea. My teachers doesn't know how to speak Korean, and my classmates are coming from countries all around the world, so we use English all the time. That is meaning that I'm getting a lot of good practice these days.

    Although I'm very happy, I'm sometimes having problems. I'm not understand my classmates' names because they don't look or sound like Korean names. I always ask the same questions: "What's your name?" and "How you spell it?" My teachers want me to call them by their first names. It's difficult for me to treat my teachers so informally, but I trying. Slowly but surely, I'm getting accustomed to my life here.

    I miss you a lot. Your still my favorite English teacher.

Hye Lee

Simple Past and Past Progressive

1 | SPELLING: REGULAR AND IRREGULAR SIMPLE PAST FORMS

Write the correct forms of the verbs.

Base Form	Simple Past
1. _____*agree*_____	agreed
2. _____	applied
3. be	_____ OR _____
4. become	_____
5. carry	_____
6. develop	_____
7. _____	ate
8. fall	_____
9. _____	felt
10. get	_____
11. grow	_____
12. live	_____
13. _____	met
14. _____	paid
15. permit	_____
16. plan	_____
17. _____	sent
18. sleep	_____

2 | SIMPLE PAST AND PAST PROGRESSIVE

Complete this magazine article. Use the correct form of the verbs in parentheses—
simple past or past progressive. Sometimes there is more than one correct answer.

First Meetings
by Rebecca Hubbard

What _____were_____ you _____doing_____
1. (do)
when you first _____ that special
2. (meet)
person in your life? A few months ago, we

_____ some couples to tell us about
3. (ask)
themselves. _____ it love at first
4. (be)

sight, or _____ you hardly _____ each other? _____
5. (notice)
you _____ out with someone else before you _____ your One True
6. (go) **7. (find)**
Love? Read some of the great stories from our readers.

Dana and I sure _____ in love at first sight! We _____ in the
8. (not fall) **9. (work)**
same office when we _____. At the time the company _____ me, she
10. (meet) **11. (hire)**
_____ to get a promotion. It _____ my first job. I _____
12. (try) **13. (be)** **14. (feel)**
scared, so I _____ to know everything. Of course Dana _____
15. (pretend) **16. (think)**
I _____ to get the promotion instead of her. One day I _____ on a
17. (want) **18. (work)**
problem when she _____ into my office. I _____ her for help at first,
19. (come) **20. (not ask)**
but I was stuck, so finally I did. And guess what! She _____ the problem! So
21. (solve)
then we _____ competing with each other and _____ in love instead.
22. (stop) **23. (fall)**

*V*an and I _____ the same high school social studies class when we
24. (take)

_____. We _____ friends right away. At the time, I _____
25 (meet)   26. (become)   27. (date)

someone else, and Van _____ interested in a romantic relationship. One day the
28. (not seem)

teacher _____ me while I _____ to Van. The teacher _____
29. (hear)   30. (whisper)   31. (get)

angry at us for talking during class, and she _____ both of us to stay after
32. (tell)

school I _____ to complain about such a severe punishment, but then I
33. (want)

_____ my mind because I _____ that staying late with a good friend
34. (change)   35. (realize)

might be fun. That afternoon, Van and I _____ talking. I was right. As soon as I
36. (not stop)

_____ with my old boyfriend, Van _____ me out.
37. (break up)   38. (ask)

*A*eesha _____ into the apartment next door when I _____ her
39. (move)   40. (see)

for the first time. I _____ on the front steps while she _____ to park a
41. (sit)   42. (try)

U-Haul moving truck in front of the apartment building. As soon as she _____
43. (jump)

out of the truck, I _____, "I'm going to marry that woman." I _____
44. (think)   45. (not ask)

her out right away because a guy _____ her move. He _____ like her
46. (help)   47. (seem)

boyfriend. One day I _____ Aleesha and her "boyfriend" in the hall. She
48. (see)

_____ me to her brother! I _____ her to dinner the next weekend.
49. (introduce)   50. (invite)

3 | EDITING

Read this entry from Aleesha's journal. There are nine mistakes in the use of the simple past and the past progressive. The first mistake is already corrected. Find and correct eight more.

December 16

                                       decided

    I'm really glad that I ~~was deciding~~ to rent this apartment. I almost wasn't move here because the rent is a little high, but I'm happy to be here. All the other apartments I looked at were seeming so small, and the neighborhoods just weren't as beautiful as this one. And moving wasn't as bad as I feared. My original plan was to take a week off from work, but when Hakim was offering to help, I didn't need so much time. What a great brother! We were moving everything into the apartment in two days. The man next door was really nice to us. On the second day, he even helped Hakim with some of the heavy furniture. His name is Jared. I don't even unpack the kitchen stuff last weekend because I was so tired. Last night I walking Mitzi for only two blocks. When I came back, Jared stood downstairs. I think I made him nervous because he was dropping his mail when he saw me. I'd like to ask him over for coffee this weekend (in order to thank him), but everything is still in boxes. Maybe in a couple of weeks . . .

Simple Past, Present Perfect, and Present Perfect Progressive

1 | SPELLING: SIMPLE PAST AND PRESENT PERFECT

Write the correct forms of the verbs.

Base Form	Simple Past	Past Participle
1. become	*became*	*become*
2. bring		
3. choose		
4. delay		
5. feel		
6. find		
7. finish		
8. get		
9. graduate		
10. hide		
11. notice		
12. omit		
13. own		
14. read		
15. reply		
16. rip		
17. show		
18. speak		

2 CONTRAST: SIMPLE PAST, PRESENT PERFECT, AND PRESENT PERFECT PROGRESSIVE

Look at the reporter's notes about the bride's and the groom's families. Then write statements about them, using the words in parentheses. Use the simple past, present perfect, or present perfect progressive form of the verbs. Add any necessary words to the time expressions. Sometimes there is more than one correct answer.

THE SKOAP-POHLIG WEDDING
BACKGROUND INFORMATION

Bride	Groom
Nakisha Skoap	Simon Pohlig
born in Broadfield	moved to Broadfield in 1997
lived here all her life	bought Sharney's Restaurant in 1999
B.A., Claremont College, 1999	basketball coach for Boys and Girls Club
1996—Began working for	2002–2004
Broadfield Examiner	author, Simon Says and Duck Soup,
2002—became crime news reporter	kids' cookbooks
and started master's degree	in Jan., started developing local
program in political science	TV show
started research on crime in	Mother—Tina Pohlig, president of
schools in Jan.	TLC Meals, Inc. for two
Father—James Skoap, joined the	years, but plans to retire soon
Broadfield Police Department	
in 1984, retired in 2004	

1. (Nakisha Skoap / live in Broadfield / all her life)

   Nakisha Skoap has lived in Broadfield all her life.

2. (she / graduate / from college / 1999)

   _____

3. (report / crime news / 2002)

   _____

4. (recently, / research / crime in schools)

   _____

5. (work / on her master's degree / 2002)

   _____

6. (her father / work / for the Broadfield Police Department / 20 years)

   _____

7. (Simon Pohlig / move / to Broadfield / 1997)

   _____

8. (own / Sharney's Restaurant / 1999)

   _____

9. (coach / basketball / for the Boys and Girls Club / two years)

   _____

10. (write / two cookbooks for children)

    _____

11. (plan / a local television show / several months)

    _____

12. (the groom's mother / serve / as the president of TLC Meals, Inc. / two years)

    _____

3 | SIMPLE PAST, PRESENT PERFECT, AND PRESENT PERFECT PROGRESSIVE

Look at Nakisha's job application. Then complete the personnel officer's notes. Use the correct affirmative or negative form of the verbs in parentheses—simple past, present perfect, or present perfect progressive. Sometimes there is more than one correct answer.

CODEX MAGAZINE
JOB APPLICATION

1. Position applied for: _____ Editor _____ Today's date: _Nov. 12, 2004_

2. Full legal name _Skoap-Pohlig_ _Nakisha_ _Ann_
         Last   First   Middle

3. Current address _22 East 10th Street_

   Broadfield,   _Ohio_   _43216_   How long at this address? _5 months_
     City   State   Zip Code

4. Previous address _17 Willow Terrace_

   Broadfield,   _Ohio_   _43216_   How long at this address? _1973–June 1, 2004_
     City   State   Zip Code

5. Education. Circle the number of years of post high school education. 1 2 3 4 5 6 ⑦ 8

6.

Name of Institution	Degree	Major	Dates Attended
1. Claremont College	B.A.	Journalism	1995–1999
2. Ohio State University	–	Urban Studies	2001
3. Ohio State University		Political Science	2002–present

   If you expect to complete an educational program soon, indicate the date and type of program.

   I expect to receive my M.S. in political science in January.

7. Current job. May we contact your present supervisor? _____ yes _×_ no

   Job Title _Reporter_   Employer _Broadfield Examiner_

   Type of Business _newspaper_   Address _1400 River Street, Broadfield, OH 43216_

   Dates (month/year) _9/96_   to (month/year) _present_

8. In your own handwriting, describe your duties and what you find most satisfying in this job.

   I am currently a crime reporter for a daily newspaper. I write local crime news.

   I especially enjoy working with my supervisor.

1. I ___have interviewed___ Nakisha Skoap-Pohlig for the editorial position.
(interview)

2. She _____ for a job on November 12.
(apply)

3. She _____ at the *Broadfield Examiner* for a long time.
(work)

4. She _____ several excellent articles for that publication.
(write)

5. She _____ that job while she _____ a college student.
(find)   (be)

6. She _____ two schools of higher education.
(attend)

7. She _____ classes at Claremont College in 1995 and _____
(begin)   (receive)

   her B.A. there.

8. Then she _____ to Ohio State University.
(go on)

9. She _____ classes in two different departments at Ohio State.
(take)

10. She _____ a master's program in urban studies.
(start)

11. She _____ a degree in urban studies, though.
(get)

12. After a year, she _____ to study political science instead.
(decide)

13. She _____ her master's degree yet.
(receive)

14. She _____ at Willow Terrace most of her life.
(live)

15. For the past five months, she _____ on East 10th Street.
(live)

16. The company graphologist _____ that we contact this applicant very soon
(recommend)

    for another interview.

17. He says that in question 8 of the application, Ms. Skoap-Pohlig _____ a space
(leave)

    between some words when she mentioned her supervisor.

18. He feels that this means she probably _____ her supervisor yet about looking
(tell)

    for a new job.

19. When Ms. Skoap-Pohlig answered question 8, she _____ her writing to either
(slant)

    the left or the right.

20. The graphologist _____ to me yesterday that this indicates that she is a clear
(explain)

    and independent thinker.

4 | EDITING

Read this letter to an advice column. There are fourteen mistakes in the use of the simple past, present perfect, and present perfect progressive. The first mistake is already corrected. Find and correct thirteen more.

Dear John,

    My son and his girlfriend have ~~made~~ *been making* wedding plans for the past few months. At first I was delighted, but last week I have heard something that changed my feelings. It seems that our future daughter-in-law has been deciding to keep her own last name after the wedding. Her reasons: First, she doesn't want to "lose her identity." Her parents have named her 31 years ago, and she was Donna Esposito since then. She sees no reason to change now. Second, she is a member of the Rockland Symphony Orchestra and she performed with them for eight years. As a result, she already became known professionally by her maiden name.

    John, when I've gotten married, I didn't think of keeping my maiden name. I have felt so proud when I became "Mrs. Smith." We named our son after my father, but our surname showed that we three were a family.

    I've been reading two articles about this trend, and I can now understand her decision to use her maiden name professionally. But I still can't understand why she wants to use it socially.

    My husband and I have been trying many times to hide our hurt feelings, but it's been getting harder. I want to tell her and my son what I think, but my husband says it's none of our business.

    My son didn't say anything so far, so we don't know how he feels. Have we been making the right choice by keeping quiet?

             A Concerned Mother Who Hasn't Been Saying One Word Yet

Past Perfect and Past Perfect Progressive

1 | SPELLING: REGULAR AND IRREGULAR PAST PARTICIPLES

Write the correct forms of the verbs.

Base Form	Present Participle	Past Participle
1. bet	betting	bet
2. _____	breaking	_____
3. cut	_____	_____
4. do	_____	_____
5. entertain	_____	_____
6. _____	_____	fought
7. forgive	_____	_____
8. lead	_____	_____
9. plan	_____	_____
10. practice	_____	_____
11. quit	_____	_____
12. _____	_____	sought
13. _____	_____	sunk
14. steal	_____	_____
15. sweep	_____	_____
16. swim	_____	_____
17. tell	_____	_____
18. _____	_____	withdrawn

2 | PAST PERFECT: AFFIRMATIVE AND NEGATIVE STATEMENTS

Read this article about Arnold Schwarzenegger. Complete the information with the affirmative or negative past perfect form of the verbs in parentheses.

Action Hero and More

Arnold Schwarzenegger is an example of what people can accomplish with determination and hard work. He was just six years old when he decided to become a famous athlete. His father

_____had taken_____ him to a special event
1. (take)

featuring Olympic swimming champion Johnny Weissmuller, and Schwarzenegger felt that one day he too would be a champion. When he first arrived in the United States in 1968, he

_____ already _____ several bodybuilding competitions in
2. (win)

Europe, but no one imagined that a bodybuilder from Austria could become a famous movie star, a successful businessman, and the governor of California.

Because Schwarzenegger _____ much English, he had a lot of problems
3. (learn)

communicating when he got to the United States. He _____ much money
4. (bring)

with him either, but that didn't stop him. Before long, he _____ a sponsor
5. (find)

so that he could continue his training as a bodybuilder, and he _____ even

_____ his own business selling supplies to other athletes. By 1970, he
6. (establish)

_____ the title of "Mr. Olympia," and some Hollywood producers
7. (earn)

_____ him the movie role of Hercules. Schwarzenegger appeared in
8. (offer)

movies and on television throughout the 1970s and continued winning bodybuilding

championships. By the time the decade was over, he _____ also

_____ a best-selling book and he _____ a B.A. in business
      9. (write)   **10. (receive)**

and international economics from the University of Wisconsin. He _____
                                                              11. (get)

married yet, but he _____ Maria Shriver, his future wife. After spending
                      12. (meet)

time with Shriver's family, Schwarzenegger got involved with the Special Olympics, an

organization founded by his mother-in-law, Eunice Kennedy Shriver, to provide sports

training and athletic competition for people with disabilities.

    Schwarzenegger achieved even greater success in the 1980s and 1990s. By the

mid-1980s, he _____ in *Conan the Barbarian* and *The Terminator*. He then
                    13. (star)

filmed action movies such as *Commando, Predator, The Running Man,* and *Red Heat.* Before

the end of the decade, Schwarzenegger _____ the first Planet Hollywood
                                                14. (open)

restaurant along with fellow action stars Bruce Willis and Sylvester Stallone. He

_____ one of the wealthiest and most popular actors in Hollywood. In the
      15. (become)

1990s, he made more action films and more comedies like *Kindergarten Cop* and *Junior.* He

also served as chairman of the President's Council on Physical Fitness, worked on other

volunteer projects, and seemed to be increasingly interested in politics.

    Before announcing his plans to run for governor of California in July 2003,

Schwarzenegger _____ filming *Terminator 3: Rise of the Machines.* He started
                    16. (finish)

his new job as California's chief executive on November 17 of that year.

    The question now is: What's next for Arnold?

3 | PAST PERFECT: *YES/NO* QUESTIONS AND SHORT ANSWERS

Look at a day in the life of a busy governor. Complete the questions about his day and give short answers. Use the past perfect.

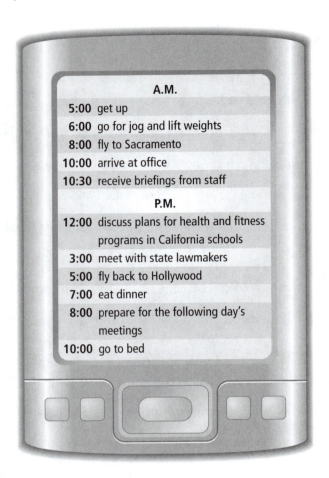

A.M.	
5:00	get up
6:00	go for jog and lift weights
8:00	fly to Sacramento
10:00	arrive at office
10:30	receive briefings from staff
P.M.	
12:00	discuss plans for health and fitness programs in California schools
3:00	meet with state lawmakers
5:00	fly back to Hollywood
7:00	eat dinner
8:00	prepare for the following day's meetings
10:00	go to bed

1. It was 6:00 A.M.

    A: _____ *Had he gotten up* _____ yet?

    B: _____ *Yes, he had.* _____

2. The governor was going for his morning jog.

    A: _____ to Sacramento yet?

    B: _____

3. It was 9:00 A.M.

    A: _____ at his office by then?

    B: _____

4. It was noon.

A: _____ briefings from his staff yet?

B: _____

5. It was shortly before 5:00 in the afternoon.

A: _____ with state lawmakers?

B: _____

6. At 6:30 in the evening, the governor arrived in Hollywood.

A: _____ dinner yet?

B: _____

7. At 10:00 P.M., he went to bed.

A: _____ for meetings the following day?

B: _____

4 | PAST PERFECT PROGRESSIVE: AFFIRMATIVE AND NEGATIVE STATEMENTS

Read the situations. Draw conclusions, using the affirmative or negative past perfect progressive form of the correct verbs from the box.

cry	do	drink	eat	laugh
listen	pay	rain	wash	~~watch~~

1. Mara wasn't in the living room, but the TV was on and there was a movie in the DVD player.

She _____*had been watching*_____ the Arnold Schwarzenegger comedy *Twins*.

2. The lights were off, and none of her schoolbooks were around.

She _____ homework.

3. The window was open, and the floor was a little wet.

It _____ .

4. There was half a sandwich on the coffee table.

Mara _____ the sandwich.

5. There was an unopened bottle of soda next to the sandwich.

She _____ the soda.

(continued)

6. Mara entered the room. There were tears on her face.

   At first I thought she _____.

7. I was wrong. Mara wasn't upset.

   She _____ really hard because of what was

   happening in the movie.

8. There was a stack of clean plates in the kitchen sink.

   She _____ dishes.

9. Mara could hear the TV from the kitchen.

   She _____ to the movie from the kitchen.

10. I was surprised when I realized how late it was.

    I _____ attention to the time.

5 | PAST PERFECT PROGRESSIVE: QUESTIONS

*A group of film students is planning the questions that they will ask a famous actor-director after he gives a lecture at their university. Use **when** and the words in parentheses to write questions with the past perfect progressive.*

1. He made his first major film. (he / dream of stardom for a long time)

   Had he been dreaming of stardom for a long time when he made his first major film?

2. He finally found an acting job. (How long / he / live in Hollywood)

   _____

3. He became a successful actor. (he / really work as a cook in a fast-food restaurant)

   _____

4. He decided to enroll in classes at the Actors Studio Drama School. (Where / he / study)

   _____

5. He began his acting classes. (Why / he / take courses in accounting)

   _____

6. He directed his first film. (How long / he / think about working behind the cameras)

   _____

7. He started his own production company. (he / look for investors for a long time)

   _____

6 | PAST PERFECT AND PAST PERFECT PROGRESSIVE

Complete this passage. Use the past perfect or past perfect progressive form of the verbs in parentheses. Use the progressive form when possible.

An Action Star of Yesteryear

Johnny Weissmuller became famous playing Tarzan in a number of movies in the 1930s and '40s. However, his first success _____*had been*_____ as a swimmer.
 1. (be)
Weissmuller was born in Romania, but he later claimed to be from a small town in western Pennsylvania— probably because he _____ to try out
 2. (decide)
for the U.S. Olympic team. He _____
 3. (swim)
for most of his life and went on to win five gold medals in the 1924 and 1928 Olympics and dozens of amateur and professional championships. When he ended his career as a swimmer, he _____ never _____ a race.
 4. (lose)
Although he _____ only small roles, Johnny Weissmuller got the role of Tarzan
 5. (have)
in the 1932 movie *Tarzan the Ape Man*. MGM studio executives _____ for an
 6. (search)
actor to star in their movie but _____ what they were looking for. Then they
 7. (not find)
heard about Weissmuller, who _____ as a swimsuit and underwear model. He
 8. (work)
got the job because of his physical appearance and abilities, not because of his acting skills.

Nevertheless, *Tarzan the Ape Man* was a hit. Audiences loved watching the adventures of the man who _____ in the jungle since he was a young boy, and they loved Johnny
 9. (live)
Weissmuller. By 1948, he _____ in a total of 12 Tarzan films. As he got older,
 10. (appear)
Weissmuller could no longer play roles like Tarzan. After he _____ movies for
 11. (make)
more than 20 years, he retired from films and went into business, but audiences still remembered him as the "King of the Jungle."

7 | SIMPLE PAST AND PAST PERFECT IN TIME CLAUSES

Look at some important events in Jennifer Lopez's life and career. Determine the correct order of the phrases below. Then combine the phrases and use the past perfect or past perfect progressive to express the event that happened first. Use the progressive form when possible. Use the simple past for the event that happened second. Add commas when necessary.

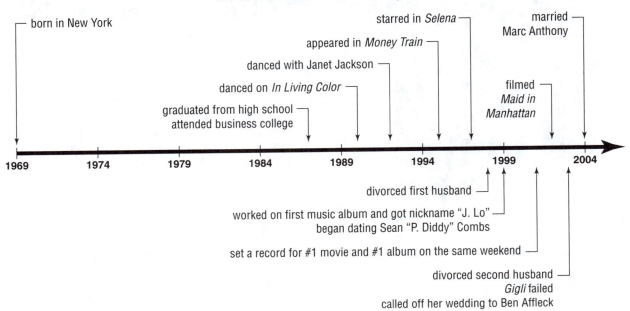

The Life and Times of Jennifer Lopez

1. briefly attended business college / graduated from high school

   After *Jennifer Lopez had graduated from high school, she briefly attended business college.*

2. became a professional dancer / studied at a business college

   Before _____

3. danced with Janet Jackson / was a dancer on the popular TV show *In Living Color*

   _____ before _____

4. appeared in her first major film / danced professionally for several years

   By the time _____

5. starred in *Selena* / finished the action film *Money Train*

   When _____ already _____

6. started her singing career / divorced her first husband

   _____ by the time _____

7. got the name "J. Lo" / made several films

   _____ before _____

8. set a record for #1 movie and #1 album on the same weekend / dated Sean "P. Diddy" Combs

   When _____

9. filmed *Maid in Manhattan* / ended her relationship with her second husband

   When _____ yet.

10. fell in love with Ben Affleck / got married twice

    By the time _____ already _____

11. called off her wedding to Ben Affleck / their movie *Gigli* failed at the box office

    _____ by the time _____

12. called off her wedding to Ben Affleck / married actor and singer Marc Anthony

    _____ after _____

UNIT

5 Future and Future Progressive

1 | CONTRAST OF FUTURE FORMS

Circle the best words to complete these conversations between two neighbors.

1. **A:** Hi, Jan. What are you doing?

   B: Packing. We'll move / (We're moving) tomorrow.

2. **A:** Do you need any help?

   B: Well, actually, I could use a hand.

   A: OK. I'll come / I'm going to come over right away.

3. **A:** Do you take / Are you taking the refrigerator?

   B: No. Our new house already has one.

4. **A:** I can't reach that vase.

   B: No problem. I'm handing / I'll hand it to you.

5. **A:** Watch out! It'll fall / It's going to fall!

   B: Don't worry. I've got it.

6. **A:** You're moving / You'll move out of state, right?

   B: Yes. To Boston.

7. **A:** Are you driving / Do you drive there?

   B: No. We'll fly / We're flying.

8. **A:** How are you getting / do you get to the airport?

   B: We're going to take / We take a taxi.

9. **A:** Oh, don't take a taxi. I'm driving / I'll drive you.

   B: Thank you! I hope we're having / we're going to have neighbors

   as nice as you in our new neighborhood!

2 | FUTURE PROGRESSIVE: AFFIRMATIVE AND NEGATIVE STATEMENTS

Complete this article. Use the affirmative or negative future progressive form of the words in parentheses.

An Old Approach to a New Problem

Next year, Azize and Kiral Yazgan _____will be moving_____
                                    1. (will / move)
from their rented two-bedroom city apartment to a place called Glenn

Commons. There they _____ in one of a
                     2. (will / live)
row of houses facing other houses, all without fences or hedges. They

_____ their car in an area in back of the houses. And even though
3. (be going to / park)

there is a nice kitchen with a large window, the Yazgans _____
                                                          4. (be going to / prepare)

dinners there. Azize, Kiral, and their two children _____ most
                                                     5. (will / eat)

evening meals along with 20 other families in a common house. And they

_____ there. They _____ along paths and
6. (will / drive)   **7. (will / walk)**

greenery.

This doesn't sound like the suburbs. What's going on? The Yazgans, along with a growing

number of other people, _____ to one of the many planned
                          8. (will / move)

communities that are now being built around the world. Called "co-housing," these

communities have cooperative living arrangements that avoid some of the isolation and

loneliness of suburban life.

While the Yazgans get to know their neighbors, they _____ also

_____ money. For starters, they _____ a
9. (will / save)   **10. (be going to / buy)**

lawn mower or a washer-dryer since the community shares large equipment. And they

_____ food, utility, or child-care bills as individuals either.
11. (be going to / pay)

Child care? The Yazgans _____ anymore about what to do when
                         12. (will / worry)

one of their children has a cold and each parent is due at a business meeting in an hour. The

center _____ for that.
       13. (will / provide)

(continued)

The Yazgans will, however, have some added responsibilities. For one thing, they will have to be much more involved in their community. Even before they move in, the couple _____ monthly meetings to decide how the community is run. And
14. (be going to / attend)
several times a month, they _____ to prepare the dinners and
15. (will / help)
_____ the child care for others. It's clearly not a lifestyle that will
16. (will / provide)
appeal to everyone.

Who started this new idea? Actually, the idea itself is quite old—going back to 19th-century European villages. Co-housing has been used in Denmark since 1972. Even though only a few co-housing communities have been completed in Canada, Europe, the United States, and New Zealand, we _____ more and more of them in the near future as
17. (be going to / see)
people try to improve the quality of their lives by returning to some of the values of the past.

3 | FUTURE PROGRESSIVE: QUESTIONS AND SHORT ANSWERS

Complete the conversations at a co-housing meeting. Use the future progressive form of the words in parentheses or short answers where appropriate.

1. **A:** When _will we be planting the garden_ _____?
   (we / will / plant the garden)
   B: Jack has bought the seeds, so we should be ready to start this week.

2. **A:** Speaking of gardening, Martha, _____?
   (you / be going to / use the lawn mower / tomorrow)
   B: _____. You can have it if you'd like.

3. **A:** You know, with more families moving in, the laundry facilities aren't adequate anymore.
   When _____?
   (we / will / get new washers)
   B: The housing committee is getting information on brands and prices. They'll be ready to report on them at the next meeting.

4. **A:** Jack, _____?
   (you / will / go to the post office / tomorrow)
   B: _____. Can I mail something for you?

5. **A:** Eun, you and Bon-Hua are in charge of dinner Friday night. What _____

_____ ?

   (you / be going to / make)

   B: How does vegetable soup, roast chicken, corn bread, salad, and chocolate chip cookies

   sound to you?

6. **A:** I really enjoyed that slide show last month. _____

_____ ?

   (the entertainment committee / will / plan anything else in the near future)

   B: _____. We're thinking of organizing a

   dance over the holidays.

7. **A:** I was just looking at my calendar. The 15th of next month is a Sunday. _____

_____ ?

   (we / be going to / meet / then)

   B: _____. We usually meet on the 15th,

   but when the 15th falls on a weekend, we switch the meeting to the following Monday.

4 | FUTURE PROGRESSIVE OR SIMPLE PRESENT

*Look at Azize and Kiral Yazgan's schedules for tomorrow. Complete the statements. Use the correct form of the verbs—future progressive with **will** or simple present.*

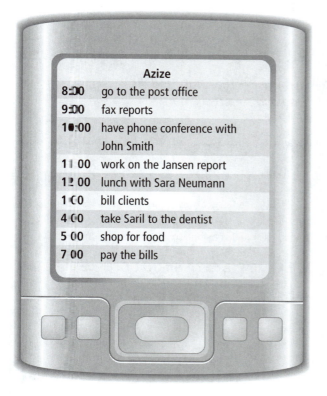

Azize	
8:00	go to the post office
9:00	fax reports
10:00	have phone conference with John Smith
11:00	work on the Jansen report
12:00	lunch with Sara Neumann
1:00	bill clients
4:00	take Saril to the dentist
5:00	shop for food
7:00	pay the bills

Kiral	
8:00	take the car in for inspection
9:00	meet with the boss
10:00	attend the time-management seminar
11:00	
12:00	lunch with Jack Allen
1:00	draft the A & W proposal
4:00	pick up the car
5:00	take Dursan to the barber
7:00	cut the grass

(continued)

1. While Azize _____ *goes to* _____ the post office,

   Kiral _____ *will be taking the car in for inspection* _____ .

2. Kiral _____ his boss

   while Azize _____ .

3. While Kiral _____ a time-management seminar,

   Azize _____ .

4. While Azize _____ lunch with Sara Neumann,

   Kiral _____ .

5. Azize _____

   while Kiral _____ the A & W proposal.

6. While Kiral _____ the car,

   Azize _____ .

7. Azize _____ food

   while Kiral _____ .

8. While Azize _____ the bills,

   Kiral _____ .

5 | EDITING

Read Kiral's note to Azize. Kiral has made seven mistakes in the use of the future and the future progressive. The first mistake is already corrected. Find and correct six more.
(Note: Sometimes there is more than one way to correct a mistake.)

> Azize—It's 8:00 p.m. now. ~~I go~~ *I'm going* to Jack's with the kids in a few
>
> minutes. We'll be play cards until 10:30 or so. While we'll play cards,
>
> Jack's daughter will be watching the kids. It will rain, so I closed all
>
> the windows. Don't forget to watch "CSI"! It'll start at 10:00. I call
>
> you after the card game because by the time we get home, you're
>
> sleeping. Enjoy your evening!
>
> Love, K

Future Perfect and Future Perfect Progressive

1 | AFFIRMATIVE AND NEGATIVE STATEMENTS

Complete this article. Use the correct form of the verbs in parentheses—future perfect or future perfect progressive.

A s of December this year, Pam and Jessica Weiner _____ *will have been working* _____ as personal
                                                                      1. (work)

time-management consultants for five years. Tired of disorganization at home, Pam

and Jessica developed a system that worked so well that they started teaching it to others. By this

anniversary celebration, hundreds of people _____
                                                                              2. (complete)

the Weiners' seminars, and these efficient sisters _____
                                                                                    3. (help)

them manage the confusion in their personal lives.

   "What a difference their seminars made!" exclaimed Corinne Smith, who completed the course a

few years ago. "This December, I _____ their
                                                                  4. (use)

system for two years. I used to do my holiday shopping on December 23. However, this year, I

_____ all my gifts by early November, and I
                        5. (buy)

_____ them too."
                6. (wrap)

   Why do we need a system? "Our lives are so complicated that we can't remember it all," explained

Pam Weiner. "A good example is a new family in our seminar. Ana and Jon have two children, they

both work, but they have no system. By Monday, they _____
                                                                                    7. (not plan)

the week's menu, and they _____ on a driving
                                              8. (not decide)

(continued)

schedule for the week's activities. That means by the time Friday comes along, they _____ probably _____ for days about

9. (argue)

these things."

The Metcalfs, one of many satisfied families, feel that their life has improved a lot since they finished the seminars. "At the end of this week, we _____

10. (not waste)

our energy arguing about who does what in the house," Aida Metcalf told us. "And we can plan for fun activities. We know that we _____ all the

11. (complete)

housework by Saturday, and we can make plans to go out. When we go back to work on Monday, we _____ a good time for two days, and we'll

12. (have)

feel refreshed."

The system also works for long-range planning. "Before the seminars, our summers were a nightmare," Aida says. "We never did the things we wanted to do. But by the end of August this year, we _____ in our community yard sale and

13. (participate)

_____ the house. And I can be sure that we

14. (redecorate)

_____ all the preparations for our September family

15. (make)

get-together."

Children enjoy using the system too. "I made a calendar for Corrie, our 12-year-old," reported Arnie Metcalf. "She loves it. By the time she gets on the school bus tomorrow morning, she

_____ several chores. For example, she

16. (do)

_____ her own room, and most likely she

17. (straighten)

_____ her own lunch as well."

18. (pack)

The Weiners are scheduled to appear on tomorrow's *Around Town*, and this also represents a kind of anniversary for them. "Our television appearances started with this show," Pam Weiner told us. "As of tomorrow, we _____ our system to

19. (explain)

television audiences for an entire year."

2 | QUESTIONS AND RESPONSES

Complete the conversations. Use the future perfect or future perfect progressive form of the words in parentheses or short answers where appropriate.

1. **A:** I'm going to the mall. Bye.

    B: I have to leave at two o'clock for a dentist appointment. _____*Will you have brought*_____
    (you / bring)

    the car back by then?

    A: _____. I don't have much to buy.

2. **A:** Corrie, your group is singing at the fund-raiser next weekend, right? By three o'clock, how

    long _____?
    (you / perform)

    B: About half an hour. Why?

    A: There's a rock band from the high school that wants to start at three.

3. **A:** This is Aida. I'm in charge of the handicrafts booth this year. How many of those nice dish

    towels _____ by Sunday? Do you know?
    (you / sew)

    B: Oh, at least 20.

4. **A:** Oh, no! I forgot about carpooling today.

    B: Suppose you leave right now. How long _____
    (the kids / wait)

    by the time you get there?

    A: Only about 15 minutes. I guess that's not a big deal.

5. **A:** Arnie, _____ downstairs by tomorrow afternoon?
    (the paint / dry)

    B: _____. We'd better give it until tomorrow night. Why?

    A: I want to hang the curtains.

6. **A:** _____ them by then?
    (the cleaners / deliver)

    B: _____. They promised me I'd have them by noon.

7. **A:** Do you realize that September first is an anniversary? That's the date we moved into this

    house.

    B: How many years _____ here?
    (we / live)

    A: Ten. Can you believe it?

3 | QUESTIONS AND AFFIRMATIVE STATEMENTS

Look at the Metcalfs' calendar for August. Write questions about their activities. Choose between the future perfect and future perfect progressive. Use the calendar to answer the questions.

AUGUST

SUNDAY	MONDAY	TUESDAY	WEDNESDAY	THURSDAY	FRIDAY	SATURDAY
1 Aida walk 1/2 mi every day	**2** Arnie paint first bedroom	**3** Arnie paint second bedroom	**4** Arnie paint bathroom	**5** Aida start driving in carpool for day camp	**6**	**7**
8 Aida water garden daily	**9** Start picking vegetables daily	**10**	**11** Arnie paint downstairs	**12**	**13**	**14**
15 Arnie finish painting indoors	**16** Arnie 4:00 P.M. dentist appointment	**17** Corrie pick blueberries for pies (need 3 quarts)	**18**	**19** Aida start baking pies for bake sale (agreed to bring 6 pies)	**20**	**21** Bake sale for fund-raiser at Community Center
22 Aida start unpacking fall clothing	**23**	**24**	**25** Iron and put away fall clothing	**26** Last day of carpool	**27**	**28**
29 Aida and Arnie pack for trip to Mom and Dad's	**30**	**31** Travel to Mom and Dad's				

1. (How many miles / Aida / walk / by August 31?)

A: *How many miles will Aida have walked by August 31?*

B: *She'll have walked 15½ miles.*

2. (How long / Aida / walk / by August 31?)

   A: _____

   B: _____

3. (How many rooms / Arnie / paint / by August 5?)

   A: _____

   B: _____

4. (How long / Arnie / paint downstairs / by August 15?)

   A: _____

   B: _____

5. (on August 16, / Arnie / leave / for his dentist appointment / by 4:00?)

   A: _____

   B: _____

6. (Aida / unpack / all the fall clothing / by August 23?)

   A: _____

   B: _____

7. (How long / Aida / drive in the carpool / by August 19?)

   A: _____

   B: _____

8. (How many quarts of blueberries / Corrie / pick / by August 19?)

   A: _____

   B: _____

9. (How many pies / Aida / bake / by August 21?)

   A: _____

   B: _____

10. (they / finish / packing for the trip / by August 31?)

    A: _____

    B: _____

UNIT

7 Negative *Yes/No* Questions and Tag Questions

1 | AFFIRMATIVE AND NEGATIVE TAG QUESTIONS AND SHORT ANSWERS

Anne-Marie wants to rent an apartment. Complete her conversations with the landlord. Use appropriate tags. Write short answers based on the apartment ad.

> N. Smithfield unfurn. 1 BR in owner occup. bldg.,
> renovated kitchen w. all new appliances, incl.
> DW, near all transp. & shopping, $500/mo. + util.
> Avail. for immed. occup. No pets. 555-7738

1. ANNE-MARIE: The rent is $500, *isn't it?* _____

   LANDLORD: *Yes, it is.* _____

2. ANNE-MARIE: That includes electricity, _____

   LANDLORD: _____

3. ANNE-MARIE: The apartment isn't furnished, _____

   LANDLORD: _____

4. ANNE-MARIE: You've renovated the kitchen, _____

   LANDLORD: _____

5. ANNE-MARIE: The kitchen doesn't have a dishwasher, _____

   LANDLORD: _____

6. ANNE-MARIE: You just put in a new refrigerator, _____

   LANDLORD: _____

7. ANNE-MARIE: A bus stops nearby, _____

   LANDLORD: _____

8. ANNE-MARIE: I can't move in right away, _____

   LANDLORD: _____

9. **ANNE-MARIE:** You won't allow pets, _____

    LANDLORD: _____

10. **ANNE-MARIE:** You live right in the building, _____

    LANDLORD: _____

2 | **NEGATIVE *YES/NO* QUESTIONS AND SHORT ANSWERS**

*Todd and a realtor are discussing two communities—North Smithfield and Greenwood. Complete their conversation. Use negative **yes/no** questions to ask about Greenwood. Write short answers based on the information in the box.*

Greenwood—Community Profile

Greenwood became a town in 1782.
Schools: Greenwood High School, Greenwood Community College
Shopping: Greenwood Mall
Transportation: local public bus
Recreational Facilities: Briar State Park, Greenwood Beach (private),
  Davis Baseball Stadium (planned for next year)
Cultural Opportunities: movie theaters (Greenwood Mall)
Average Rent: $678

---

1. **REALTOR:** North Smithfield has a community college.

    TODD: *Doesn't Greenwood have a community college?* _____

    REALTOR: *Yes, it does.* _____

2. **REALTOR:** North Smithfield built a public beach.

    TODD: _____

    REALTOR: _____

3. **REALTOR:** There's an airport in North Smithfield.

    TODD: _____

    REALTOR: _____

4. **REALTOR:** You can see live theater performances in North Smithfield.

    TODD: _____

    REALTOR: _____

(continued)

5. REALTOR: People in North Smithfield shop at a nearby mall.

   TODD: _____

   REALTOR: _____

6. REALTOR: The average rent in North Smithfield is under $700.

   TODD: _____

   REALTOR: _____

7. REALTOR: North Smithfield has been a town for more than a hundred years.

   TODD: _____

   REALTOR: _____

8. REALTOR: They're going to build a baseball stadium in North Smithfield.

   TODD: _____

   REALTOR: _____

3 | NEGATIVE *YES/NO* QUESTIONS AND TAG QUESTIONS

Complete the conversations. Use the correct form of the verbs in parentheses. Write negative **yes/no** *questions and tag questions.*

A.   Ari: ____*Didn't*____ you ____*move in*____ last week?
                                    1. (move in)

     Dan: Yes. You haven't been living here very long yourself, ____*have you*____?
                                                                  2.

     Ari: Oh, it's been about a year now.

     Dan: It's a nice place to live, _____?
                                      3.

     Ari: We think so.

B. Katie: You haven't seen the letter carrier this morning, _____?
                                                             1.

     Dan: No. Why?

   Katie: I don't think our mail is being forwarded from our old address.

     Dan: _____ you _____ one of those
                                         2. (fill out)

          change-of-address forms?

   Katie: Yes. But that was almost a month ago. We should be getting our mail by now,

          _____?
              3.

     Dan: I would think so.

C. Dan: _____ there an all-night supermarket nearby?
   1. (be)

   Mia: Yes. It's at 10th and Walnut.

   Dan: I know where that is. _____ there

   _____ a restaurant there?
   2. (used to / be)

   Mia: That's right. It closed last year.

   Dan: That's strange. It hadn't been there very long, _____?
   3.

   Mia: About a year. I guess the location just wasn't good for a restaurant.

D. Ari: The new neighbors are really friendly, _____?
   1.

   Mia: Yes. That reminds me. The people across the hall invited us over for coffee and cake on

   Saturday afternoon. You haven't made any plans for then, _____?
   2.

   Ari: Well, I was going to work on our taxes.

   Mia: _____ you _____ a little break?
   3. (can / take)

   Ari: Sure. Why not?

4 | NEGATIVE *YES/NO* QUESTIONS AND TAG QUESTIONS

*The new tenants are going to visit their neighbors. They want to confirm some of the assumptions they have. Read their assumptions. Then write negative **yes/no** questions or tag questions. For some sentences, both types of questions are possible. (Remember: The only time you can use negative **yes/no** questions is when you think the answer is "Yes.")*

1. We think the people in Apartment 4F have lived here a long time.

   The people in Apartment 4F have lived here a long time, haven't they?

   OR

   Haven't the people in Apartment 4F lived here a long time?

2. I don't think our apartment had been occupied for a while.

   Our apartment hadn't been occupied for a while, had it?

3. We believe this is a good building.

   _____

4. It seems that the owner takes good care of it.

   _____

(continued)

5. It looks like he has just finished renovations on the lobby.

   _____

6. We don't think that he painted our apartment before we moved in.

   _____

7. I have the impression he doesn't talk very much.

   _____

8. I don't think the rent will increase next year.

   _____

9. It looks like some new people will be moving into Apartment 1B.

   _____

10. We have the impression that this is a really nice place to live.

    _____

So, Too, Neither, Not either, and But

1 | AFFIRMATIVE AND NEGATIVE ADDITIONS

This is a true story about twin sisters. Complete the story with affirmative and negative additions.

A Birthday Surprise

Tamara Rabi and Adriana Scott are twin sisters who were born in Guadalajara, Mexico. However, the twins didn't meet until shortly after their 20th birthday.

Tamara and Adriana were adopted and grew up in different parts of New York. Adriana's adoptive mother knew that her daughter had a twin, _____*but*_____ Tamara's mother _____*didn't*_____. When Tamara began her studies at Hofstra
1.   2.
University, a fellow student said that she looked really familiar, and _____
3.
did another and then another. At her 20th birthday party, one of the guests told her about his friend Adriana. Adriana was from Mexico, and Tamara was _____.
4.
Adriana didn't know her birth parents, and _____ did Tamara. Adriana's
5.
parents had adopted their child as an infant, and so _____ Tamara's. The
6.
most surprising thing of all was that the two girls had the same birthday. Tamara was intrigued. She decided to contact Adriana by e-mail several days after the party.

(continued)

Adriana and Tamara found that they were not exactly alike. For example, Tamara likes Chinese food, _____ Adriana doesn't. Because she had worn braces, Adriana's teeth are straight, but Tamara's _____. Still, they share many similarities, and when they exchanged photographs, they couldn't believe how much they resembled each other. The twins agreed to meet.

On the day of their meeting, Tamara didn't want to go, and Adriana _____ either. They were both afraid of what might happen next, but Adriana had invited friends to come along, _____ so had her sister. Having their friends there made them feel safe.

Shortly after their 20th birthday, the twins were reunited. Adriana received a wonderful gift, and her sister did _____: They received the gift of each other!

2 | AFFIRMATIVE OR NEGATIVE?

Complete the conversations with affirmative and negative additions and responses.

A. **Kaleb:** I've heard that there's a twins festival every year.

   Karen: _____*So have*_____ I.
                1.

   Kaleb: I didn't realize that there were enough twins around to have a festival.

   Karen: I _____. But hundreds of them attended the festival last year.
                  2.

   Kaleb: I'm talking about the festival in Twinsburg, Ohio.

   Karen: I _____. Did you know that some of the people who go there actually
                  3.
       fall in love and get married?

  Kaleb: Are you kidding?

  Karen: No. In 1998, Diane Sanders and her twin sister Darlene went to the festival in

       Twinsburg, and Craig Sanders and his brother Mark _____. Diane and
                          4.

       Craig fell in love, and _____ Darlene and Mark.
                5.

Kaleb: Let me guess. Their children are twins.

Karen: Not exactly. Diane and Craig have identical twin sons, _____ Darlene and Mark _____. They have two singletons—one daughter was born in 2001 and the other in 2003.

6.

Kaleb: What's a singleton?

Karen: A child that isn't a twin.

B. **Ellie:** I thought I knew where the expression "Siamese twins" came from, _____ I _____. I had to look it up.

1.

Grant: What did you find out?

Ellie: Well, you know it refers to identical twins whose bodies are joined. Chang and Eng Bunker were conjoined twins who were born in Siam in 1811. The term was originally used to describe them. The preferred term today is "conjoined twins."

Grant: I remember reading about them. Most doctors at the time had never seen conjoined twins, and _____ anyone else. Chang and Eng became famous.

2.

Ellie: It's interesting. They ended up living in the United States. Chang got married, and _____ Eng. Their wives were sisters. Chang and his wife had 10 children, and Eng and his wife had 11.

3.

Grant: Do you know how they died?

Ellie: When they were older, Chang was sick, _____ Eng _____. He was still strong and healthy. One night Eng woke up, and his brother was dead. Eng died the same night.

4.

C. **Kim:** More and more women in the United States are having children later in life.

Amy: Women in Europe _____. The average age of new mothers is rising there.

1.

Kim: Because of the fact that new mothers are older and because of fertility treatments, the number of triplets, quadruplets, and quintuplets will continue to increase.

Amy: And _____ the number of twins.

2.

3 | AFFIRMATIVE OR NEGATIVE

Look at this information about twins festivals. Then complete the sentences about the festivals. Use the information in parentheses to write appropriate additions and responses.

Twins Festivals			
LOCATION	**Twinsburg, Ohio, U.S.A**	**Pleucadeuc, France**	**Beijing, China**
YEAR STARTED	1976	1994	2004
TIME OF YEAR	first week of August	mid-August	first week of October
WHO ATTENDS	twins, triplets, quads, quints, and their families	twins, triplets, quads, quints, and their families	twins and the general public
TYPES OF EVENTS	talent show, parade, contests, food, fireworks, photos	music, parade, photographs, food	entertainment, social events
COST	$15, additional costs for triplets, quads, and quints	free	free
REGISTRATION	recommended	recommended	none required

1. Twinsburg, Ohio, has a twins festival each year, ___*and so does Pleucadeuc, France* OR *and Pleucadeuc, France, does too*___ .
   (Pleucadeuc, France)

2. Twinsburg was holding its festival in the 1980s, _____ .
   (Pleucadeuc)

3. Pleucadeuc doesn't charge an entrance fee, _____ .
   (Beijing)

4. The Twinsburg festival isn't free, _____ .
   (the Pleucadeuc and Beijing festivals)

5. Twinsburg will celebrate its festival next year, _____ .
   (Pleucadeuc)

6. Twinsburg festival participants should register, _____ .
   (participants at Pleucadeuc)

7. The Pleucadeuc festival doesn't have a talent show, _____ .
   (the Beijing festival)

8. Twinsburg schedules its festival for August, _____ .
   (Pleucadeuc)

9. Twins pay $15 at the Twinsburg festival, _____ .
   (triplets, quads, and quints)

10. Pleucadeuc didn't sponsor a festival in 1990, _____ .
    (Beijing)

11. Twins have gone to the Twinsburg festival for many years, _____ .
    (their families)

Gerunds and Infinitives: Review and Expansion

1 | GERUND OR INFINITIVE?

Complete these statements with the correct form—gerund or infinitive—of the verb **watch.**
(Note: In some cases, both the infinitive and the gerund will be correct.)

1. The children wanted _____*to watch*_____ television.

2. I suggest _____*watching*_____ television.

3. We would like _____ television.

4. Do you need _____ television?

5. I was busy, so I really couldn't afford _____ television.

6. I should have stopped, but I continued _____ television.

7. Has a teacher ever encouraged you _____ television?

8. Some people dislike _____ television.

9. Others absolutely refuse _____ television.

10. Please turn off all the lights after you finish _____ television.

11. What time did you start _____ television?

12. My sister is addicted. She can't help _____ television.

13. How long ago did you quit _____ television?

14. Do you mind _____ television?

15. My roommate and I have decided _____ television.

16. I feel like _____ television.

17. They considered _____ television.

18. He keeps _____ television.

19. When you're tired, you seem _____ television.

20. Are they going to the movies or planning _____ television?

2 | GERUND OR INFINITIVE?

Use the correct form—gerund or infinitive—of the verbs in parentheses to complete this article.

TOO ANGRY ___to remember___ THE COMMERCIALS?
1. (remember)

According to a new study, _____ violent
2. (watch)

TV shows makes it difficult _____ brand
3. (recall)

names or commercial messages. Violence creates anger,

and instead of _____ the commercials,
4. (hear)

viewers are attempting _____ themselves
5. (calm)

down after violent scenes. The conclusion: _____ violent programs may not
6. (Sponsor)

be profitable for advertisers.

This conclusion is good news for the parents, teachers, and lawmakers who are

struggling _____ the amount of violence on U.S. television. They had a small
7. (limit)

victory in the late 1990s, when lawmakers and the television industry designed a TV-

ratings system. Unfortunately, Congress did not ask parents _____ in
8. (participate)

_____ the system, and the industry does not invite parents _____
9. (create) **10. (preview)**

shows before it assigns ratings. As a result, parents are still guessing about the content of

the shows their kids watch.

Why are parents objecting to _____ violence in television shows? The
11. (have)

numbers tell the story: A typical child will see 8,000 murders and 100,000 acts of violence

between the ages of 3 and 12! It's impossible _____ that this input won't
12. (believe)

affect young children. In fact, researchers have noted the following possible effects of

_____ this much violence:
13. (view)

1. Children may become less sensitive to other people's suffering.

2. They may also become fearful of _____ with other people.
14. (interact)

3. They may be more likely _____ in a way that is harmful to others.
15. (behave)

Studies have shown that a majority of people want commercial TV _____
16. (produce)
more educational and informational programs. In addition, more than 75 percent prefer

_____ the number of hours of TV that children watch, and the American
17. (limit)
Academy of Pediatrics recommends _____ children _____ more
18. (not permit)   19. (watch)
than one to two hours per day.

It's hard _____ why the entertainment industry resists _____
20. (understand)   21. (make)
changes. Parents, teachers, and doctors are urging the industry _____ clearer
22. (develop)
ratings and _____ violence in children's shows. What's more, violent TV
23. (get rid of)
shows don't seem _____ companies an effective way _____ their
24. (offer)   25. (advertise)
products. Even artists in the television business feel that it's time _____ the
26. (decrease)
amount of violence in American TV shows and have warned the industry executives

_____ _____ change.
27. (not continue)   28. (avoid)
The industry may choose _____ attention to the public, but it will not be
29. (not pay)
able to ignore Congress. Lawmakers want _____ the way networks market
30. (investigate)
violent shows to teenagers. They are also asking the industry _____ violence-
31. (schedule)
free hours, when no violent content is allowed. Hopefully, parents in the United States will

someday feel good about _____ the family TV.
32. (turn on)

3 | GERUND OR INFINITIVE?

*A TV talk-show host is talking to a doctor about children and TV violence. Complete the
interview with the appropriate word or phrase from the boxes plus the gerund or infinitive
form of the verb in parentheses.*

fed up with	likely	~~shocked~~	unwilling	used to

HOST: I was _____*shocked to learn*_____ that children will see 100,000 acts of violence on
1. (learn)
television before they are 12. I had no idea it was that bad. It also appears that the

networks are _____. They seem pretty satisfied with things the
2. (change)
way they are.

(continued)

DOCTOR: Yes, I think that they're _____ all the responsibility on the

3. (put)

viewer. That's the way it's always been, and they're accustomed to it.

HOST: The networks may not want to change, but I know a lot of us are really very

_____ violence during family viewing times. We're really sick of

4. (see)

it. A lot of my friends don't even turn on the cartoons anymore.

DOCTOR: That's probably a good idea. Several studies show that children are more

_____ others after they watch violent cartoons. It's really quite

5. (hit)

predictable.

| decide | dislike | force | hesitate | stop |

HOST: OK. Now what can we do about this problem?

DOCTOR: Well, viewers can make a big difference. First of all, we have to put a lot of pressure on

the networks and _____ them _____ shows more clearly.

6. (rate)

They'll give in if enough viewers tell them they must.

HOST: What else?

DOCTOR: When you see something you don't like, pick up the phone immediately. Don't wait. We

shouldn't _____ the networks about material that we find

7. (tell)

offensive. Recently a network _____ a violent ad for another

8. (run)

show right in the middle of a family sitcom. So many people complained that they

reversed that decision and _____ the ad in that time slot.

9. (show)

HOST: Violence bothers my kids, but they _____ a show once it starts.

10. (turn off)

They want to stick it out to the end.

| consider | forbid | insist on | permit |

DOCTOR: Parents have to assert their authority and _____ the channel

11. (change)

when violence appears. Sometimes they'll face a lot of resistance, but they should

be firm.

HOST: You know, in a lot of families, parents work until six. They can't successfully

_____ their children _____ certain

                                          12. (turn on)

shows. They're just not around to enforce the rules.

DOCTOR: There's help from the electronics industry in the form of a V-chip.

HOST: What exactly is a V-chip?

DOCTOR: It's a chip built into television sets. The V-chip doesn't _____

children _____ violent shows. It blocks them electronically.

                       13. (tune in)

HOST: It sounds like something all parents should _____.

                                                  14. (own)

advise	agree	hesitate	keep

HOST: Is there anything else that you _____ parents _____?

                                          15. (do)

DOCTOR: Parents must _____ with their children. They shouldn't

                            16. (communicate)

_____ their kids about their feelings and opinions—and

           17. (ask)

especially about their activities.

HOST: Thank you, Doctor, for _____ to us today.

                                    18. (speak)

4 | **OBJECTS WITH GERUNDS AND INFINITIVES**

Read the conversations about watching television. Then use the correct forms of the words in parentheses to write summaries.

1. KIDS: Can we watch TV now?

   MOM: I'm sorry, but you have to finish your homework first.

   SUMMARY: _____ *Their mother didn't allow them to watch TV.* _____

                         (their mother / allow / they / watch TV)

2. ANNIE: My parents finally bought me a new TV, but it has a V-chip.

   BEA: What's that?

   ANNIE: It's something that blocks violent shows so that I can't watch them.

   SUMMARY: _____

                         (a V-chip / interfere with / Annie / watch violent shows)

(continued)

3. ROGER: Our kids really seem to like *Reading Rainbow.*

    CORA: I know. It's so great that there's a high-quality TV show about reading and learning.

    SUMMARY: _____
    (Reading Rainbow / encourage / they / get interested in books)

4. DAD: You were having some pretty bad nightmares last night, Jennifer. I think you'd better stop watching those cop shows.

    JENNIFER: OK, but I really love them.

    SUMMARY: _____
    (her father / tell / Jennifer / watch cop shows / anymore)

5. STUDENTS: We want to watch the TV news, but the reporting on adult news shows is usually really frightening.

    TEACHER: Try *Nick News with Linda Ellerbee.* It's a great news show for kids.

    SUMMARY: _____
    (the teacher / recommend / they / watch Nick News)

6. SUE: I'll never forget that great Knicks game we watched last year.

    BOB: What Knicks game?

    SUE: Don't you remember? We saw it together! The Knicks beat the Rockets 91–85.

    SUMMARY: _____
    (Bob / remember / they / see that game)

7. FRED: Does Sharif still watch *Z-Men* every Saturday?

    ABU: No. We explained that it was too violent for him, and he decided not to watch it anymore.

    SUMMARY: _____
    (Sharif's parents / persuade / he / watch Z-Men)

8. MOM: Sara, it's nine o'clock. Time to turn off the TV.

    SARA: Oh, Mom. Just a little longer, OK?

    MOM: You know the rules. No TV after nine o'clock.

    SUMMARY: _____
    (the mother / insist on / Sara / turn off the TV)

9. AZIZA: This is boring. What's on the other channels?

    BEN: I don't know. Where's the remote control?

    SUMMARY: _____
    (Aziza / want / Ben / change the channel)

10. NICK: *Primer Impacto,* my favorite TV news program, starts in five minutes.

    PAUL: I've never understood why you watch that show. It's in Spanish, and you don't speak Spanish at all.

    SUMMARY: _____
    (Nick / can't get used to / Paul / watch a Spanish-language news program)

5 | EDITING

Read this student's essay. There are eleven mistakes in the use of the gerund and infinitive. The first mistake is already corrected. Find and correct ten more.

Asoka Jayawardena
English 220
May 30

Violence on TV

        hearing
I'm tired of ~~hear~~ that violence on TV causes violence at home, in school, and on the streets. Almost all young people watch TV, but not all of them are involved in committing crimes! In fact, very few people choose acting in violent ways. To watch TV, therefore, is not the cause.

Groups like the American Medical Society should stop making a point of to tell people what to watch. If we want living in a free society, it is necessary having freedom of choice. Children need learn values from their parents. It should be the parents' responsibility deciding what their child can or cannot watch. The government and other interest groups should avoid to interfere in these personal decisions. Limiting our freedom of choice is not the answer. If parents teach their children respecting life, children can enjoy to watch TV without any negative effects.

10 Make, Have, Let, Help, and Get

1 | CONTRAST: *MAKE, HAVE, LET, HELP,* AND *GET*

Complete this article about the roles that animals can play in our lives. Circle the correct verbs.

The Animal-Human Connection

Can pets get / (help) humans lead better lives? Not only animal lovers but also some
1.

health-care professionals believe that pets <u>let / get</u> us improve our quality of everyday living.
2.

Pets <u>have / help</u> their owners stay healthy. For example, dogs need daily exercise, and
3.

this <u>has / makes</u> many owners turn off their television sets or computers and go outside for
4.

a walk. While walking their dogs, they receive the health benefits of being physically active,

and they are able to talk to the people they see on the street or in the park. These positive

human relationships <u>get / make</u> dog owners feel happy, which can lead to longer, healthier
5.

lives. Speaking of positive relationships, it is interesting to note that research shows pet

owners often have lower blood pressure as a result of spending time with their animals. It

seems that pets <u>get / make</u> their owners to relax.
6.

Animals can also play an important role for humans who are sick. In some cases,

health-care professionals <u>let / have</u> animals provide
7.

attention, affection, and companionship for their patients.

The animals don't replace other forms of medical care,

but they <u>help / have</u> patients recover more quickly and live
8.

longer. The Delta Society is a nonprofit organization that

promotes the idea of using animals in places such as hospitals, nursing homes, and

rehabilitation centers. The society <u>lets / gets</u> volunteers to work with those in need, but it
9.

doesn't <u>let / make</u> just any pet participate in its programs. It <u>makes / gets</u> pets and their
10. **11.**

owners complete training courses so that the animals will be friendly and give comfort to

the humans they meet.

   In addition to helping those who are ill, animals can assist people with disabilities.

Guide dogs <u>help / make</u> people who are blind cross busy streets or take public
12.

transportation. People who are unable to move their arms or legs can <u>help / have</u> their dogs
13.

open doors, turn lights off and on, and even answer the telephone. Special hearing dogs

<u>make / let</u> hearing-impaired owners pay attention when the doorbell rings, their baby cries,
14.

or a fire alarm sounds.

---

2 | *MAKE, HAVE, LET, GET,* AND *HELP* + OBJECT + CORRECT FORM OF THE VERB

*Read this tip sheet from an animal welfare agency. Complete the sentences by adding
pronoun objects and the correct form of the verbs in parentheses.*

Dogs Are Family Members, Too

Whether your family has a dog or you'd like to bring a dog

into your home, here are some things to consider.

If you're thinking about getting a dog . . .

*   It takes time and money to care for a dog. Be sure that you have enough of both. A dog could be a

    member of your family for 15 years or more.

*   Talking to everyone in your family will make _____*them feel*_____ part of the decision-
    1. (feel)

    making process, and they'll be more likely to welcome a dog as a new member of the family.

*   Pets are not always welcome. Find out if your landlord will let _____ a dog
    2. (keep)

    in your apartment.

(continued)

- There are always animals available for adoption. Before buying a dog from a pet shop or a breeder, contact your local animal shelter. At the shelter, ask about classes or an adoption program that will help

  _____ what kind of dog is best for you and your family. Also talk to staff
  3. (decide)

  members about the health and history of a dog that you want to adopt. It's a good idea to have

  _____ you as much information as possible.
  4. (give)

If there are children in the family . . .

- Your child may really want a dog, and she may promise to take care of your family's new pet, but

  honestly, it may be impossible to get _____ it. Consider dividing pet care
  5. (do)

  responsibilities among all members of the family, including children. Depending on the children's ages,

  it's certainly possible to have _____ specific tasks such as taking the dog
  6. (take care of)

  for a walk after school or giving the dog food and water.

- Children may have to learn to be gentle. Get _____ animals need respect
  7. (realize)

  just like humans, and that means no hitting, kicking, riding, or pulling the tail of the family dog.

- At some point, your dog will get overexcited when he is playing. Children should know what to do to get

  _____.
  8. (calm down)

- It pays to be careful. If you have a very young child, she may love the family pet, but never let

  _____ with the family dog alone. Adult supervision is essential.
  9. (play)

If there is a new baby coming into the family . . .

- Your dog will know that there's been a change, and he will probably be excited, anxious, and

  curious. It's up to you to help _____. Before the baby arrives, introduce
  10. (adjust)

  him to baby sounds. He should also get accustomed to seeing a baby, so use a doll or let

  _____ time around a real infant if possible.
  11. (spend)

- Your dog may need training so that you can get _____ you at all times
  12. (obey)

  when he is around the new baby.

- Although you'll be busy with your new baby, spending time with your dog will make

  _____ that he is still an important member of the family. It will also help
  13. (understand)

  _____ during this very busy time in your life.
  14. (relax)

If you want to know more, contact our organization and let _____ you with
15. (provide)

more detailed information on dogs and families.

3 | AFFIRMATIVE AND NEGATIVE STATEMENTS

Read the conversations. Then use the correct forms of the verbs in parentheses to complete the summaries. Add pronouns when necessary.

1. JOHN: Mom, can I get a horse?

   MOTHER: No, of course you can't get a horse!

   SUMMARY: John's mother _____ *didn't let him get a horse.* _____
   (let)

2. MOTHER: Instead of a horse, will you agree to adopt a dog or a cat?

   JOHN: OK.

   SUMMARY: John's mother _____
   (get)

3. MOTHER: You can make the choice.

   JOHN: I'd rather have a cat.

   SUMMARY: His mother _____
   (let)

4. MOTHER: Now, you have to do some research on pet care.

   JOHN: I can do that. I know a couple of animal-protection groups that have good information on their websites.

   SUMMARY: She _____
   (make)

5. JOHN: Do I have to do all of the research by myself?

   MOTHER: Yes, you do.

   SUMMARY: John's mother _____
   (help)

6. JOHN: I found out that I have to be 18 to adopt a pet. Can you fill out and sign the adoption application forms for me?

   MOTHER: Sure.

   SUMMARY: John _____
   (get)

7. MOTHER: First, you have to explain the adoption process to me.

   JOHN: I have all of the information right here.

   SUMMARY: John's mother _____
   (have)

8. JOHN: I have enough money to pay the adoption fees.

   MOTHER: You may need the money later. I'll pay the fees.

   SUMMARY: John's mother _____
   (make)

4 | EDITING

Read this university student's e-mail. She made seven mistakes in the use of **make**, **have**, **let**, **help**, *and* **get**. *The first mistake is already corrected. Find and correct six more.*

Hi, Ami!

Thanks for staying in touch. Your e-mails always make me ~~to~~ smile—even when I'm feeling

stressed. Knowing that I have a good friend like you really helps me relax and not take

things so seriously. My classes are difficult this semester. I still can't believe that three of my

professors are making them write 20-page papers.

At the end of last semester, my roommates and I decided to get a dog. Actually, my

roommates made the decision and then got me go along with it. I made them promise to

take care of the dog, but guess who's doing most of the work! Don't misunderstand me. I

love Ellie and appreciate what a great companion she is. I take her for a walk every morning

and every night and make her run and play in the park near our apartment as often as I can

because I know how much she enjoys it. Still, I wish I could have my roommates to spend

just an hour a week with "our" dog. At this point, I can't even get them feeding Ellie, and now

they want to move to an apartment complex that won't let us to have a dog. I think I'm going

to have to choose whether to live with my roommates or with Ellie—and I think I'm going to

choose Ellie!

Take care. I'll write again soon.

Neha

Phrasal Verbs: Review

1 | PARTICLES

Complete the phrasal verbs with particles from the box. You will use some particles more than once.

ahead	back	down	off
on	out	over	up

Phrasal Verb	**Meaning**
1. catch _____on_____	*become popular*
2. cheer _____	*make someone feel happier*
3. do _____	*do again*
4. get _____	*make progress, succeed*
5. let _____	*allow to leave*
6. let _____	*disappoint*
7. look _____	*examine*
8. pick _____	*select or identify*
9. take _____	*return*
10. try _____	*use to find out if it works*
11. turn _____	*raise the volume*
12. turn _____	*lower the volume*
13. use _____	*consume*
14. write _____	*write on a piece of paper*
15. put _____	*delay*
16. think _____	*invent*

2 | PHRASAL VERBS

Read about New Year traditions around the world. Complete the article with the correct forms of the phrasal verbs in the box. Choose the verbs that are closest in meaning to the words in parentheses.

burn up	cut down	get together	give out	go back	go out
~~pay back~~	put on	put together	set up	throw away	

Starting New

Wearing new clothes, _____*paying back*_____
              1. (repay)

debts, lighting candles—many cultures share similar

New Year traditions. In Iran, for example, people

celebrate *Now Ruz*, or New Day, on the first day of

spring. A few days before the festival, families

_____ bushes and _____ piles of wood. They
  2. (bring down by cutting)   **3. (assemble)**

set the piles on fire, and before the wood _____ , each family
                             4. (burn completely)

member jumps over one of the fires and says, "I give you my pale face, and I take your red

one." The day before the New Year begins, the family _____ a table
                               5. (prepare for use)

in the main room with special foods and objects, such as colored eggs, cake, and the *haft-sin*,

seven objects with names beginning with the sound "s." Everyone _____
                               6. (cover the body with)

new clothes, and the family _____ around the table. When the New
              7. (meet)

Year begins, family members hug each other and _____ gifts,
                         8. (distribute)

especially to the children. For the next 12 days, people visit each other, but on the 13th day,

it is unlucky to be inside a house, so people _____ and spend the day
                         9. (leave)

in parks and fields, where they have picnics, listen to music, and play sports. They don't

_____ home until sunset. At the end of the day, everyone
  10. (return)

" _____ " bad luck by throwing wheat or lentils into a river.
    11. (discard)

3 | PHRASAL VERBS AND OBJECTS

Complete the conversations with the phrasal verbs and objects in parentheses. Place the object between the verb and the participle when possible.

A. Vijay: We need about two dozen candles for *Diwali*.

Nira: I'll _____ *pick them up* _____ after work.
1. (pick up / them)

Vijay: While you're there, why don't you get some new decorations?

Nira: Let's have the children _____. You know how
2. (pick out / them)

excited they get about the Hindu New Year.

B. Eva: Why do you _____
1. (empty out / the money and everything else in your pockets)

on *Rosh Hashana*?

Simon: It's a custom for the Jewish New Year to throw what's in our pockets into moving

water. It's like getting rid of last year's bad memories.

Eva: Here's my cigarette lighter. I'd love to _____.
2. (throw away / it)

C. May: When will we _____ for the Chinese New Year?
1. (set off / the firecrackers)

Ning: Not until dark.

May: Don't the firecrackers have something to do with evil spirits?

Ning: Yes. We believe that the noise _____.
2. (keep away / them)

D. Liam: Are you decorating for Christmas?

Zoé: No, we're _____ for Kwanzaa, the African-American
1. (hang up / these streamers)

harvest celebration. It comes at the same time as Christmas and New Year.

Liam: What is your mom putting on the table?

Zoé: That's a *kinara*. We _____ to hold the Kwanzaa candles.
2. (set up / it)

E. Kelsey: Do you usually make New Year's resolutions?

Ian: Yes, and I _____
1. (write down / all of the resolutions that I make each year)

because they're so easy to forget by February.

Kelsey: This year I'd like to stop eating desserts.

Ian: I _____ for a few months last year. I lost five pounds.
2. (gave up / them)

4 | EDITING

Read this person's list of New Year's resolutions. There are eleven mistakes in the use of phrasal verbs. The first mistake is already corrected. Find and correct ten more.

<u>New Year's Resolutions</u>

Wake ~~out~~ ^{up} earlier. (No later than 7:30!)

Work out at the gym at least 3 times a week.

Lose 5 pounds. (Give over eating so many desserts.)

Be more conscious of the environment:

—Don't throw down newspapers. Recycle them.

—Save energy. Turn on the lights when I leave the apartment.

Straighten up my room:

—Hang out my clothes when I take off them.

—Put my books back where they belong.

—Give some of my old books and clothing that I no longer wear away.

Don't put off doing my homework assignments. Hand in them on time!

Read more.

Use the dictionary more. (Look over words I don't know.)

When someone calls and leaves a message, call them back right away. Don't put off it!

Get to know my neighbors. Ask them for coffee over.

Phrasal Verbs: Separable and Inseparable

1 | PARTICLES

Complete the phrasal verbs with the correct particles.

Phrasal Verb	**Meaning**
1. call _____ back _____	*return a phone call*
2. get _____	*recover from an illness or a bad situation*
3. cross _____	*draw a line through*
4. call _____	*cancel*
5. drop _____	*visit unexpectedly*
6. look _____	*be careful*
7. keep _____	*continue*
8. talk _____	*persuade*
9. blow _____	*explode*
10. turn _____	*reject*
11. run _____	*meet accidentally*
12. put _____	*return to its original place*
13. work _____	*solve*
14. go _____	*continue*
15. find _____	*discover*
16. turn _____	*lower the volume*

2 | PHRASAL VERBS

Complete these paragraphs with the appropriate form of the phrasal verbs from the boxes.

catch on	~~come out~~	figure out	go off	help out
take away	team up with	turn off	turn on	

A. There have been a lot of changes since the first consumer

cell phones _____*came out*_____ in the 1980s.
_{1.}

The original phones were big, heavy, and very expensive.

After designers _____ how to
_{2.}

make them smaller and more affordable, they really began

to _____. Now, people all over
_{3.}

the world are _____ their mobile
_{4.}

phones and using them in ways that could never have been imagined in the 1980s. Several

years ago, wireless companies _____ digital-photography experts to
_{5.}

produce camera phones, which are now popular with consumers. Internet access is another

way that cell phones _____ us _____ by
_{6.}

keeping us connected and informed. However, there is a negative side to wireless technology.

For example, when cell phones _____ in restaurants, movie theaters,
_{7.}

and classrooms, they can be annoying. When we're forced to listen to other people's

conversations in public places, it _____ our privacy and
_{8.}

the privacy of the person talking on the phone. Clearly, it's sometimes best to

_____ our cell phones _____.
_{9.}

end up	find out	keep up with	look over
pick out	put away	use up	watch out for

B. Cell phones let us _____ friends and family whenever and wherever

we want, but they can _____ being very expensive. It's great to stay
                              2.

in touch, but it's hard to know when to stop talking and _____ our

mobile phones _____. Cell phone companies advertise reasonably
                        3.

priced calling packages, but it's easy to _____ all the minutes on a
                                                  4.

basic plan. Many of us have _____ the hard way what it's like to pay
                                      5.

overage charges. Smart consumers do comparison shopping and _____
                                                                            6.

wireless service with features such as free weekend and evening minutes, unlimited calls to

family members, and no roaming charges when customers go out of their calling area. Smart

consumers also _____ their cell phone contract carefully before they
                        7.

sign it. They realize how important it is to _____ hidden fees.
                                                      8.

3 | PHRASAL VERBS AND OBJECT PRONOUNS

Complete the conversations. Use phrasal verbs and pronouns.

1. LUIS: I thought you were going to ask the Riveras over for dinner.

   INES: I did. I _____ *asked them over* _____ for Friday night.

2. LUIS: Did you invite their son too? He gets along well with Jimmy.

   INES: That's a good idea. He really does _____.

3. INES: If you run into Marta tomorrow, invite her too. She knows the Riveras.

   LUIS: I usually don't _____ on Tuesdays. If we want her to come,

   we should call.

4. INES: I'd like you to straighten up your room before the Riveras come over.

   JIMMY: No problem. I'll _____ as soon as I come home from school

   Friday.

(continued)

5. **JIMMY:** There's a big game on TV at eight o'clock on Friday that I'd like to watch. Do we really have to get together with the Riveras on Friday?

   INES: Yes, we do. We haven't _____ since last summer. Besides, we canceled our dinner plans last month, and I don't want to cancel again.

6. **INES:** Maybe you could pick out some CDs to play during dinner.

   JIMMY: Sure. I'll _____ right now.

7. **INES:** I hope we can count on the Riveras to bring the dessert.

   LUIS: Don't worry. You can _____. If they promised to bring dessert, then they'll bring it.

8. **INES:** You can bring out the roast now. It's done.

   LUIS: Great. I'll _____ right away so we can eat. It smells great.

9. **INES:** Be careful! Don't pick up the pan without pot holders! It's hot!

   LUIS: Ow! Too late! I just _____.

10. **LUIS:** I'm going to turn down the music. It's a little too loud.

    INES: Oh, don't get up. I'll _____.

11. **LUIS:** Should I cover up the leftovers?

    INES: Uh-huh. Here's some aluminum foil. After you _____, you can put them in the refrigerator.

12. **INES:** You didn't eat much at dinner tonight. You're really sticking to your diet, aren't you?

    LUIS: That's right. I've _____ for three weeks now, and I plan to continue until I lose 15 pounds.

13. **INES:** Could you help me put away these folding chairs?

    LUIS: Why don't you rest? I'll _____.

14. **INES:** Don't forget to turn on the dishwasher before you go to bed.

    LUIS: I'll _____ now. That way I won't forget.

15. **INES:** Good night. I'm going to bed and try to figure out that crossword puzzle that's been giving me trouble.

    LUIS: Good luck! Let me know when you _____.

4 | DEFINITIONS

See if you can figure out this puzzle.

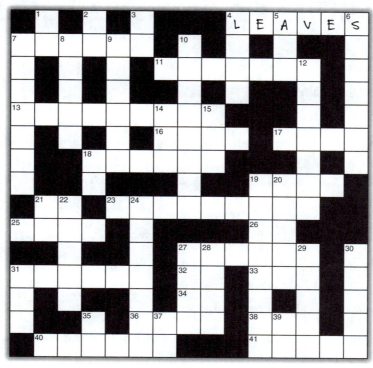

Across

  4. Gets off (the bus)
  7. Want
 11. Mix up
 13. Figure out
 16. Opposite of *fall*
 17. Leave out
 18. Think up
 19. These can run out of ink.
 21. _____ it rains, it pours.
 23. Call up
 25. Don't go away. Please _____.
 26. Street *(abbreviation)*
 27. Middle
 31. Call off
 32. Indefinite article
 33. Professional *(short form)*
 34. Medical doctor *(abbreviation)*
 36. What time _____ she usually show up?
 38. Negative word
 40. Take place
 41. Put up (a building)

Down

  1. Pick _____ up at 5:00. I'll be ready then.
  2. Hello
  3. You and I
  4. Pick up
  5. Advertisements *(short form)*
  6. Hands in
  7. Talk over
  8. Tell off
  9. Take back
 10. Carry on
 12. Look over
 14. *am, is,* _____
 15. Eastern Standard Time *(abbreviation)*
 18. Drop _____ on
 19. Put off
 20. Come in
 21. The music is loud. Please turn _____ down.
 22. Pass out
 24. Blow up
 27. Her book _____ out last year.
 28. Marcia always _____ up with more work than anyone else.
 29. Rte. *(full word)*
 30. *Drop in* means "to _____ unexpectedly."
 31. You put a small bandage on it.
 35. Don't guess. Look it _____.
 37. Please go _____. Don't stop.
 39. Either . . . _____

13 Adjective Clauses with Subject Relative Pronouns

1 | RELATIVE PRONOUNS

In many countries, people sometimes try to meet others through personal ads in magazines and newspapers. Circle the correct relative pronouns to complete these ads.

Best Friends—I'm a 28-year-old man (who) / which enjoys reading, baseball, movies, and long
                                      1.

walks in the country. You're a 20-to-30-year-old woman <u>who / whose</u> interests are compatible with
                                                        2.

mine and <u>who / whose</u> believes that friendship is the basis of a good marriage. **7932** ✍️
          3.

Starstruck—You remind me of Johnny Depp, <u>who / that</u> is my favorite actor. I remind you of a
                                              4.

movie <u>who / that</u> is fun and full of surprises. Won't you be my leading man as we dance across the
       5.

screen of life? **3234** ☎

Where Are You?—35-year-old career-oriented female <u>that / which</u> relaxes at the gym and
                                                      6.

<u>who / whose</u> personality varies from philosophical to funny seeks male counterpart. **9534** ✍️ ☎
  7.

Forever—Are you looking for a relationship <u>who / that</u> will stand the test of time? Call this 28-year-
                                                8.

old male <u>who / which</u> believes in forever. **2312** ☎
          9.

Soul Mates?—The things <u>that / who</u> make me happy are chocolate cake, travel, animals, music,
                            10.

and someone <u>whose / who</u> ideas of a good time are similar to mine. **1294** ✍️
             11.

Enough Said—I want to meet a guy <u>who / whose</u> is smart enough to read, active enough to run
                                      12.

for a bus <u>that / who</u> just left the stop, silly enough to appreciate Adam Sandler, and mature enough
           13.

to want a commitment. I'm a 25-year-old female <u>who / which</u> finds meaning in building a
                                                14.

relationship and then a family. **6533** ✍️

2 | SUBJECT–VERB AGREEMENT

Read the results of a study about the ingredients of a happy marriage. Complete the information with appropriate relative pronouns and the correct form of the verbs in parentheses.

What It Takes to Have a Happy Marriage

ABILITY TO CHANGE AND ACCEPT CHANGE

Successful couples are those _____*who*_____
<u>1.</u>

_____*are*_____ able to adapt to changes
<u>2. (be)</u>

_____ _____ within the marriage
<u>3.</u>   <u>4. (occur)</u>

or in the other partner. People _____ _____ happily married see
<u>5.</u>   <u>6. (stay)</u>

themselves "as free agents _____ _____ choices in life."
<u>7.</u>   <u>8. (make)</u>

ABILITY TO LIVE WITH THE UNCHANGEABLE

They can live with situations _____ _____. They accept the
<u>9.</u>   <u>10. (not change)</u>

knowledge that there are some conflicts _____ _____
<u>11.</u>   <u>12. (remain)</u>

unsolvable. This attitude relates to life in general. According to the study, people

_____ marriages _____ to an end because of a crisis such as an
<u>13.</u>   <u>14. (come)</u>

illness or job loss tend to be individuals _____ _____ unable to
<u>15.</u>   <u>16. (be)</u>

deal with the realities of life. Their only answer is to end the relationship.

ASSUMPTION OF "FOREVER"

Most newlyweds believe their marriage is "forever." This is an important belief

_____ _____ the relationship survive problems.
<u>17.</u>   <u>18. (help)</u>

TRUST

In marriage, trust allows for the sense of security _____ _____
<u>19.</u>   <u>20. (make)</u>

long and satisfying relationships possible. It is the glue _____
<u>21.</u>

_____ the marriage together.
<u>22. (hold)</u>

(continued)

ENJOYING EACH OTHER'S COMPANY

According to the study, "Although they may spend evenings quietly together in a room, the

silence _____ _____ them is the comfortable silence of two
          23.   24. (surround)

people _____ _____ they do not have to talk to feel "close."
          25.   26. (know)

They can simply enjoy being together.

SHARED HISTORY

A marriage is a relationship _____ _____ a reality and history of
          27.   28. (have)

its own. People in good marriages value their shared history and gain strength from it. They

keep it alive with family stories and photos.

LUCK

What role does luck play? You need luck in choosing a partner _____
          29.

_____ the ability to change and trust and love. You need luck, too, in the type
     30. (have)

of family you come from. Research suggests that families _____ members
                            31.

_____ warm and supportive provide good preparation for future relationships.
     32. (be)

You also need luck with life itself. This is often a question of attitude. According to the study,

"Couples _____ _____ themselves lucky are the ones
          33.   34. (consider)

_____ _____ luck where they are able to." They don't wait for
          35.   36. (seize)

luck to come to them.

---

3 | SENTENCE COMBINING

Combine the pairs of sentences. Make the second sentence in each pair an adjective clause.
Make any other necessary changes.

1. I met Rebecca in 1994. Rebecca is now my wife.

   I met Rebecca, who is now my wife, in 1994.

2. She was visiting her favorite aunt. Her aunt's apartment was right across from mine.

   _____

3. I was immediately attracted to Rebecca because of her smile. The smile was full of warmth and good humor.

   _____

4. I could see that Rebecca was a terrific woman. Her interests were similar to mine.

   _____

5. Ballroom dancing was one of our favorite activities. Ballroom dancing was very popular in those days.

   _____

6. We also enjoyed playing cards with some of our close friends. Our friends lived in the neighborhood.

   _____

7. Our friend Mike taught us how to ski. Mike was a professional skier.

   _____

8. We got married in a ski lodge. The ski lodge was in Vermont.

   _____

9. Our marriage has grown through the years. Our marriage means a lot to us both.

   _____

10. The love and companionship have gotten stronger. The love and companionship make us very happy.

    _____

11. Even the bad things have brought us closer together. Bad things have happened.

    _____

12. I really love Rebecca. Rebecca is not only my wife but also my best friend.

    _____

14 Adjective Clauses with Object Relative Pronouns or *When* and *Where*

1 | RELATIVE PRONOUNS AND *WHEN* AND *WHERE*: SUBJECT AND OBJECT

Circle the correct words to complete these book dedications and acknowledgments.

A.

> To my family, (which) / that has given me my first world, and to my friends, who / whom have
>
> **1.**   **2.**
>
> taught me how to appreciate the New World after all.

(Eva Hoffman, *Lost in Translation: A Life in a New Language.* New York: Penguin, 1989.)

B.

> I'd like to thank everyone which / who has been in my life. But since I can't, I'll single out a few
>
>   **1.**
>
> who / whose   were particularly helpful to me in the writing of this book . . . thanks to my loving and
>
> **2.**
>
> amazingly patient wife, Dianne, to all our friends whom / which we couldn't see while I was mired
>
>   **2.**
>
> in self-examination, and to my family.

(Ben Fong-Torres, *The Rice Room.* New York: Hyperion, 1994.)

C.

> My book would not have been written without the encouragement and collaboration of
>
> many people. I should like to thank my wife, who / that has seen little of me at home
>
>   **1.**
>
> during the last few years, for her understanding. . . . I should like to thank the NASA
>
> personnel at Houston, Cape Kennedy, and Huntsville, which / who showed me around
>
>   **2.**
>
> their magnificent scientific and technical research centers . . . all the countless men and
>
> women around the globe whose / whom practical help, encouragement, and
>
>   **3.**
>
> conversation made this book possible.

(Erich Von Däniken, *Chariots of the Gods?* New York: G.P. Putnam, 1977.)

D.

I ask the indulgence of the children <u>who / whose</u> may read this book for dedicating it to a
grown-up. I have a serious reason: he is the best friend I have in the world. I have another
reason: this grown-up understands everything, even books about children. I have a third
reason: he lives in France, <u>which / where</u> he is hungry and cold. He needs cheering up. If all
these reasons are not enough, I will dedicate this book to the child from <u>whom / who</u> this
grown-up grew. All grown-ups were once children—although few of them remember it.

(Antoine de Saint-Exupéry, *The Little Prince*. New York: Harcourt Brace, 1943.)

E.

The field-work on <u>which / that</u> this book is based covers a span of fourteen years, 1925–1939; the
thinking covers the whole of my professional life, 1923–1948. . . . It is impossible to make articulate . . .
the debt I owe to those hundreds of people of the Pacific Islands <u>who / whose</u> patience, tolerance of
differences, faith in my goodwill, and eager curiosity made these studies possible. Many of the children
<u>whom / which</u> I held in my arms and from <u>whom / whose</u> tense or relaxed behavior I learned lessons
<u>who / that</u> could have been learned in no other way are now grown men and women; the life they live in
the records of an anthropologist must always have about it a quality of wonder both to the
anthropologist and to themselves. . . .

(Margaret Mead, *Male and Female*. New York: William Morrow, 1949.)

F.

Nearly every person interviewed for this book has been given relevant portions of the
manuscript to check for errors, but any mistakes remain my responsibility. Conversations and
events <u>who / that</u> I did not hear or see have been reported as the participants remembered
them. . . . Much has been written about the decline of American education. It is a joy to
describe one place <u>where / when</u> that shaky institution has experienced an unmistakable
revival. . . . I hope this book will impart some of that excitement to any <u>which / who</u> wish to
set forth in the same direction as Jaime Escalante and the many other teachers in America
like him.

(Jay Mathews, *Escalante: The Best Teacher in America*. New York: Henry Holt, 1988.)

(continued)

G.

> . . . some contributions to my work come from people I have never met and probably never will. I am grateful . . . to the citizens of the city of Portland and the county of Multnomah, Oregon, <u>which / whose</u>
> **1.**
> taxes support the Multnomah County Library, without <u>whom / whose</u> reference material this book would
> **2.**
> not have been written. I am also grateful to the archaeologists, anthropologists, and other specialists
> <u>who / whom</u> wrote the books from <u>which / that</u> I gathered most of this information for the setting and
> **3.**   **4.**
> background of this novel. . . . There are many who helped more directly . . . Karen Auel, <u>that / who</u>
> **5.**
> encouraged her mother more than she ever knew . . . Cathy Humble, of <u>which / whom</u> I asked the
> **6.**
> greatest favor one can ask of a friend—honest criticism—because I valued her sense of words.

(Jean M. Auel, *The Clan of the Cave Bear*. New York: Crown, 1980.)

2 | RELATIVE PRONOUNS AND *WHEN* AND *WHERE*: OBJECT

Read this article about book dedications and acknowledgments. Complete the information with **who(m)**, **which**, **that**, **whose**, **when**, *or* **where**, *and the correct forms of the verbs in parentheses.*

> *To L. F., without* _____*whose*_____ *encouragement . . .*
>   **1.**
>
> Dedication and acknowledgment pages are the places _____ an author
>   **2.**
>
> _____ the people _____ support and assistance he or she
> **3. (thank)**   **4.**
>
> _____ valuable while writing. These words of gratitude are probably the last
> **5. (find)**
>
> ones _____ the author _____ for a book, but they'll be the
>   **6.**   **7. (write)**
>
> first ones _____ a reader _____. This fact may explain some
>   **8.**   **9. (read)**
>
> of the problems _____ writers _____ when writing these
>   **10.**   **11. (face)**
>
> pages. The thanks should be gracious and well written, but the task of writing them most often
>
> comes at the end of a long project—a time _____ an author sometimes
>   **12.**
>
> _____ words. In the 16th and 17th centuries, _____ rich
> **13. (run out of)**   **14.**
>
> nobles _____ artists, writers were paid well for writing dedications in
>   **15. (support)**
>
> _____ they _____ their wealthy employers. Some "authors"
> **16.**   **17. (praise)**
>
> made a profession of dedication writing. They traveled the countryside with fake books into
>
> _____ they _____ a new dedication at each rich family's house.
> **18.**   **19. (insert)**

A modern writer usually dedicates a book to a family member, friend, or colleague with

_____ he or she _____ deeply connected. The dedication
　　　　20. 　　　　　　　　　　　　　**21. (feel)**

page is short and often contains only the initials of the person to _____ the
　　　　　　　　　　　　　　　　　　　　　　　　　　　　　　22.

author _____ the work. In the acknowledgments, _____ the
　　　　23. (dedicate)　　　　　　　　　　　　　　　　　　　　　　　**24.**

author _____ more room, everyone from reference librarians to proofreaders
　　　　25. (have)

is thanked.

　　Unfortunately, most writers' handbooks give authors very little help with dedications and

acknowledgments. "It's just something _____ you _____
　　　　　　　　　　　　　　　　　　　　26.　　　　　　　　　　　**27. (be supposed to)**

know how to handle," complains one author.

3 | RELATIVE PRONOUNS, *WHERE,* AND *WHEN*

Combine the pairs of sentences, using **who(m), which, that, whose, where,** *or* **when.** *Make the second sentence in each pair an adjective clause. Make any other necessary changes.*

1. Jean M. Auel wrote a novel. I enjoyed reading it.

    Jean M. Auel wrote a novel which I enjoyed reading.

2. *The Clan of the Cave Bear* tells the story of a clan of prehistoric people. Auel started researching the book in 1977.

    _____

3. It took a lot of work to learn about these prehistoric people. Auel wanted to understand the prehistoric people's lives.

    _____

4. The clan lived during the Ice Age. Glaciers covered large parts of the earth then.

    _____

5. The people lived near the shores of the Black Sea. There are a lot of large caves there.

    _____

6. The clan made their home in a large cave. Bears had lived in the cave.

    _____

(continued)

7. The task of hunting had great importance in the life of the Cave Bear Clan. The men were responsible for the task of hunting.

_____

8. One aspect of their lives was their technical skill. Auel describes that aspect well.

_____

9. She learned some of the arts. Prehistoric people had practiced them.

_____

10. In her preface, Auel thanks a man. She studied the art of making stone tools with him.

_____

11. She also thanks an Arctic survival expert. She met him while she was doing research.

_____

12. He taught her to make a snow cave on Mt. Hood. She spent one January night there.

_____

13. She went through a difficult time. She couldn't write then.

_____

14. A fiction writer inspired her to finish her book. She attended the writer's lecture.

_____

15. Jean Auel's novel remains popular with fans around the world. She published the novel in 1980.

_____

4 | OPTIONAL DELETIONS OF RELATIVE PRONOUNS

In five of the sentences in Exercise 3, the relative pronoun can be deleted. Rewrite the sentences below with the relative pronoun deleted.

1. _Jean M. Auel wrote a novel I enjoyed reading._ _____

2. _____

3. _____

4. _____

5. _____

5 | EDITING

Read this student's book report. There are nine mistakes in the use of adjective clauses. The first mistake is already corrected. Find and correct eight more.

Jorge Ramos

English 220

    For my book report, I read *The Clan of the Cave Bear*, ~~that~~ *which* Jean M.
Auel wrote after several years of research. In this novel about the life
of prehistoric people, the main character is Ayla. She is found by a
wandering clan after an earthquake kills her family. The same earthquake
destroyed the cave in which this clan had lived, and they are searching
for another home. The clan leader wants to leave Ayla to die. She is an
Other—a human which language and culture his clan doesn't understand.
However, the leader's sister Iza, Ayla soon calls Mother, adopts her.

    The story takes place at a time where human beings are still
evolving. Ayla is a new kind of human. Her brain, which she can use it to
predict and make plans, is different from Iza's and other clan members'.
Their brains are adapted to memory, not new learning, whom they fear and
distrust. At first, Ayla brings luck to the clan. She accidentally
wanders into a place where they find a large cave, perfect for their new
home. She is educated by Iza, who's great knowledge everyone respects.
The skills that Iza passes on to Ayla include healing and magic, as well
as finding food, cooking, and sewing. However, Ayla's powers make it
impossible for her to stay with the clan. She learns to hunt, a skill
where women are forbidden to practice. Her uncle, that she loves very
much, allows her to stay with the clan, but after he dies, she loses his
protection. Another earthquake, for which she is blamed, destroys the
clan's home, and she is forced to leave.

UNIT 15 Modals and Similar Expressions: Review

1 | MODALS: FUNCTION

Read the sentences. What do they express? Choose from the functions in the box.

ability	advice	assumption
future possibility	necessity	prohibition

1. You ought to start your homework now.   *advice*

2. I have to watch *Animal World* for my science class. _____

3. I may write a report about crocodiles. _____

4. *Animal World* must be on now. It's 8:00. _____

5. That can't be a log. It must be a crocodile. _____

6. We must handle the captured animal carefully. _____

7. You must not try this yourselves. _____

8. That show was great. Should I type my report? _____

9. The show might go off the air next season. _____

10. I couldn't tape *Big Cat* last week because the DVD recorder was broken. _____

11. I can't watch this show. My parents don't allow it. _____

12. You'd better buy a new DVD recorder. _____

13. You could get an A for this report. It's really good. _____

14. Were you able to download photos for your report? _____

15. We shouldn't stay up too late. _____

2 | AFFIRMATIVE AND NEGATIVE STATEMENTS

Complete this article with the correct affirmative or negative form of the verbs in parentheses.

THE CROCODILE HUNTER

At his sixth birthday party, Steve Irwin

_____ *had to be* _____ the happiest little boy in
1. (have to / be)

Australia. His parents had just given him the present he'd

really wanted—a 10-foot-long snake. You

_____ surprised, therefore, to learn
2. (may / be)

that Steve's parents were also animal lovers. In 1970, when Steve was eight, Bob and Lyn Irwin

_____ their dream—and Steve's—and move to rural Queensland,
3. (be able to / fulfill)

where they opened a reptile park called Australia Zoo. By the following year, nine-year-old

Steve _____ crocodiles by diving into rivers—even at night! Steve's
4. (could / catch)

parents never said, "You _____ on those crocodiles, son." In fact, Bob
5. (had better / jump)

was right in there with Steve, teaching him the fine art of crocodile wrestling.

Today, Steve shares his love of animals with his wife, Terri, and his two children, Bindi Sue

and Robert. On any given day, visitors to Australia Zoo _____ the
6. (might / see)

Irwin family hard at work there. In addition, fans of the Irwin family

_____ them on the popular TV show *The Crocodile Hunter*. The show
7. (can / watch)

_____ like a serious show, but it is. Steve and Terri are very committed
8. (may / sound)

to protecting the crocodile. In the show, Steve wrestles and captures crocodiles that are living

too close to humans. People are afraid because these big crocodiles _____
9. (could / harm)

them, but Steve is afraid that people _____ the crocodiles. After he
10. (might / shoot)

captures a crocodile, he carefully moves it farther into the wilderness. In these high-tech times,

Steve _____ wrestling to capture the crocodiles. There are other ways.
11. (have to / use)

(continued)

But, Steve explains, by wrestling them, he _____ them with fewer

           12. (be able to / catch)

injuries (to the crocs, that is). And Steve believes, more than anything else, that we

_____ all wild animals, even the ones that _____

    13. (should / take care of)   **14. (might / mind)**

having us for dinner.

3 | MODALS: MEANING

Read these conversations between two people getting ready to go to a nature preserve.
Circle the correct words to complete the conversations.

1. **A:** We might / can't be away for a week. Is this enough food?

   B: Maybe not. Let's pack a little more.

2. **A:** Should / Might we drive around in the nature preserve?

   B: We 'd better / 'd better not. The roads are bad. Let's take the boat with us.

3. **A:** We 've got to / don't have to leave before dark. I don't know the way.

   B: We can / shouldn't leave when I finish fixing the boat engine.

4. **A:** Do you think it's going to rain?

   B: It may / may not. I don't see any clouds.

5. **A:** The brochure says that visitors must not / don't have to build fires. It's too dangerous.

   B: Then I ought to / shouldn't buy fuel for the stove so that we can cook safely.

6. **A:** This ought to / has to be the worst engine I've ever worked on.

   B: Maybe we should / can't take the canoe instead.

   A: You may / must not be right. The canoe is quieter too.

7. **A:** We 'd better not / might not forget the camera this time.

   B: I know. Last year, we weren't able to / can't take pictures of that crocodile.

8. **A:** I hear the phone. Who could / should that be?

   B: It must / couldn't be the kids. I told them to call before we left.

9. **A:** You 'd better / may not remind Kate to feed the dog for us.

   B: You're right. She's so busy, she couldn't / might not remember.

10. **A:** Oh, well. We can / must always call her on the cell phone and remind her.

    B: How were we able to / did we have to survive without cell phones?

11. **A:** Mom, you 've got to / 'd better not wear boots. There are snakes out there.

    B: You cannot / don't have to worry. We're always careful.

12. **A:** Did I turn off the stove? I just can't / may not remember.

    B: Maybe we shouldn't / should check the house one more time.

    A: OK, but then we could / have got to leave. It's really getting late.

4 | EDITING

Read this letter to Steve Irwin. There are nine mistakes in the use of modals. The first mistake is already corrected. Find and correct eight more.

151 Split Oak Lane
Richmond, VA 23237
January 15, 2006

Dear Mr. Irwin:

    I have watched all of your shows several times, and I must ~~to be~~ *be* one of your biggest fans. The first time I saw you stick your hand in a nest of poisonous snakes, I might not believe my eyes. In fact, some people have come to the conclusion that you ought to be crazy to take risks like that. But they still don't able to stop watching! Since your show started, you can make a lot of people interested in nature. I am one of them.

    I am a high school senior, and because of your shows, I might major in zoology in college. I'm going to take general courses the first two years, so I must not choose my major yet. One of my concerns is that there couldn't be any jobs in zoology when I graduate. What is your opinion? Will there be a lot of jobs in this field in the next few years? My other problem is that my parents don't want me to work with animals. They haven't actually said, "You don't have to major in zoology," but they are very worried. What can I to tell them? I hope you will be able to find the time to answer this letter.

Sincerely,

An Wang

An Wang

UNIT 16 — Advisability in the Past

1 | QUESTIONS AND RESPONSES: AFFIRMATIVE AND NEGATIVE STATEMENTS

Complete this article with the correct form of the verbs in parentheses or with short answers. Choose between affirmative and negative.

I ___Shouldn't Have Said___ *That!*
1. (should / say)

(Or, How to Stop Fighting Losing Battles)

All families argue, but when you've just had the same argument for the tenth or hundredth time, it's time to stop and think. Why are you stuck? What _____ you _____ this time to make things different? For this week's column, we asked
2. (could / do)
Dr. Iva Gripe to answer some questions that readers frequently ask. Dr. Gripe is an expert in resolving family conflicts.

Q: My husband promised to help around the house more. A week after his promise, his stuff was all over the living room again. I pointed it out, and we had an argument. _____ I _____ it pass and not said anything?
3. (Should / let)

A: _____. Real change takes much more time. After just a week, you
4.
_____ him a break. I suggest waiting 30 days before bringing up the
5. (could / give)
subject again.

★ ★ ★ ★ ★

Q: My wife just bought a very expensive camera. I felt she _____ it with
6. (might / discuss)
me first, but I didn't want to start a fight. Instead, I decided not to buy some clothes I need. I don't feel comfortable with that decision. How _____ I _____ this
7. (should / handle)
situation instead?

A: Your feelings tell you that you _____ to your wife's problem. You're
8. (should / adjust)

right. Adjusting only makes the situation worse. Instead, you _____ her,
9. (ought to / face)

and you _____ to find a solution together. (But see the previous
10. (should / try)

question and answer. Don't expect miracles right away!)

★ ★ ★ ★ ★

Q: Yesterday, my wife had an argument with her boss. I gave her a lot of good advice, but she didn't

take it, and I felt insulted. _____ I _____ her problem, or what?
11. (Should / ignore)

A: _____. Ignoring your wife wouldn't have been the answer. Next time,
12.

try to find out what she wants from you. Maybe she just wants you to listen quietly. She really

_____ you, but since she didn't, try asking directly.
13. (ought to / tell)

★ ★ ★ ★ ★

Q: I always make out the checks and pay the bills. Last month I asked my husband to do it because I

was busy. He did, but he was angry about it. I feel that he _____ more
14. (might / act)

pleasantly, but I didn't say anything. _____ I _____?
15. (Should / complain)

A: _____. You were right not to say anything. Remember: You asked him
16.

to pay the bills, and he did. You didn't ask him to be nice about it.

★ ★ ★ ★ ★

Q: My husband spends every weekend in front of the TV. He ignores me and the children, and we all

feel bad about that. Last Sunday I called him a couch potato. What's our problem? I think we

_____ solve this before now.
17. (ought to / be able to)

A: Sure, he _____ the entire day in front of the TV. But remember: It takes
18. (should / spend)

two to make a problem. For your part, you definitely _____ him an
19. (should / call)

insulting name. Name-calling just makes the situation seem permanent. Instead, you

_____ on your own feelings about the situation. You
20. (might / focus)

_____ to him that his behavior makes you feel insecure and ignored,
21. (could / admit)

for example.

2 | AFFIRMATIVE AND NEGATIVE STATEMENTS

Look at these pointers for resolving conflicts in families. Write sentences about each situation. Use the words in parentheses and the language from the chart.

Conflicts That Nobody Loses		
Situation	**Do . . .**	**Don't . . .**
One of you is a saver, and one is a spender. You fight about money.	• create a budget with some "personal money" for each partner. • treat your partner's attitudes with respect.	• deny your purchases. • accuse your partner of irresponsibility.
You dislike spending time with your spouse's family.	• plan ahead and schedule time alone with each other.	• sulk. • pretend to be sick.
Your child won't clean up his or her room.	• start with small tasks. • provide containers to help organize the toys.	• expect 100 percent change overnight. • yell. • give up and do it yourself.

1. When Tom's wife asked him about a new shirt, he said it wasn't new.

   Tom shouldn't have denied his purchase.
   <u>   </u>
                           (should / deny)

2. Cora and Tom planned a budget without any spending money for either of them.

   _____
                       (ought to / create)

3. When Cora refused to spend money on a new TV, Tom called her a cheapskate.

   _____
                       (might / treat)

4. When Tom bought a new TV anyway, Cora told him he was irresponsible.

   _____
                       (should / accuse)

5. On Friday, Kayla and Josh hadn't decided what they were going to do on the weekend. Josh suggested visiting his parents.

   _____
                       (should / plan)

6. By Sunday, they hadn't spent any time alone together.

   _____
                       (could / schedule)

7. On Saturday, at Kayla's sister's house, Josh wouldn't talk to anybody.

   _____
                       (should / sulk)

8. Hakeem's room was a mess. His parents told him to clean the whole room immediately, and Hakeem was very upset.

_____

(might / start)

9. Hakeem didn't know where to put his toys.

_____

(could / provide)

10. Hakeem's father cleaned it up himself on Saturday.

_____

(should / give up / do)

3 | EDITING

Read this college student's journal entry. There are nine mistakes in the use of modals. The first mistake is already corrected. Find and correct eight more.

> shouldn't
> I think my new roommate and I have both realized our mistakes. Reggie ~~should~~ have demanded the biggest room in the apartment as soon as he arrived. He ought have spoken to me first—after all, I've lived here longer than he has. On the other hand, I really shouldn't shout at him as soon as he asked me. I could have control my temper and just talked to him about the problem first. I felt really bad about that—until he invited friends over the night before I had to take a test! Then I got so angry, I couldn't sleep. He might have asks me first! I oughta have said something right away, but I didn't want to yell again. Of course, some of my habits make Reggie mad too. For example, I could've started washing my dishes when he moved in, but I just let them pile up in the sink. That was pretty gross—I definitely shouldn't have did that. But should have he dumped all the dirty dishes in my bedroom? He might found a better way to tell me he was annoyed. Last week, he wanted to talk about our problems. As soon as we started, I realized we should have talked much sooner. Things have worked out a lot better since our discussion.

1 | DEGREES OF PROBABILITY

Circle the correct words to complete this high school student's notes about the ancient Maya.

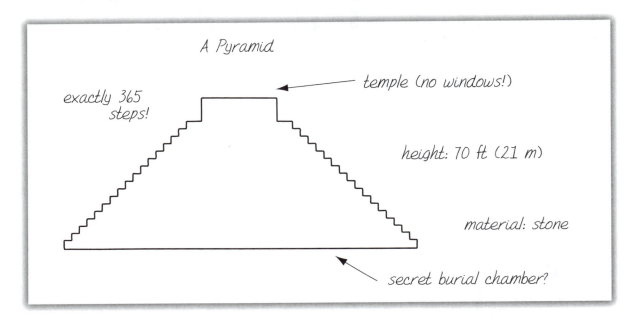

A Pyramid

exactly 365 steps!

temple (no windows!)

height: 70 ft (21 m)

material: stone

secret burial chamber?

1. It must have / might have taken many years to build a pyramid.

2. It couldn't have / might not have been easy without horses or oxen.

3. The temples must have / could have been very dark inside.

4. Some pyramids must have / may have had a secret burial chamber.

5. The Maya must have / could have had some knowledge of astronomy.

   Look at the number of steps!

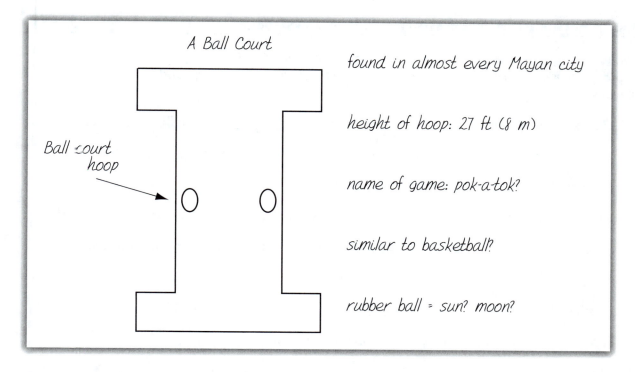

A Ball Court

Ball court hoop

found in almost every Mayan city

height of hoop: 27 ft (8 m)

name of game: pok-a-tok?

similar to basketball?

rubber ball = sun? moon?

6. The Maya <u>must have / might have</u> enjoyed this sport.

7. The name of the game <u>must have / could have</u> been *pok-a-tok*.

8. It <u>must have / may have</u> been similar to basketball.

9. The solid rubber ball the Maya used <u>must have / could have</u> symbolized the sun or the moon.

10. The average Mayan man was 5 feet 1 inch (1.52 m) tall. It <u>couldn't have / might not have</u> been very easy to get the ball into the hoop.

11. The rules of the game were complicated. It <u>had to have / might have</u> been very difficult to score.

2 | AFFIRMATIVE AND NEGATIVE STATEMENTS

Who were the ancient Maya? What happened to their advanced civilization? Complete these speculations with the verbs in parentheses. Choose between affirmative and negative.

1. The ancient Maya _____*must have been*_____ very intelligent people. They had
   (must / be)

   developed the most complex writing system in the Western Hemisphere as well as an

   amazingly accurate astronomical calendar.

2. In the 1990s, archaeologists found four new Mayan sites in thick mountain jungle on the

   Yucatán Peninsula in Central America. Because of the thick jungle growth, the sites

   _____ easily visible.
   (must / be)

3. Archaeologists _____ very excited by the discovery. It
   (had to / feel)

   provided a lot of important information about the Maya.

4. The Maya _____ the sites between the years 700 and 900.
   (must / occupy)

   The style of architecture and the pottery found at the sites are typical of that time.

5. The sites lie between two major population centers. The ancient residents

   _____ with these cities.
   (may / trade)

6. Archaeologists once thought the Maya _____ in the city
   (could / live)

   centers. They believed that the centers were used only for ceremonial purposes.

7. Archaeologists used to believe that the ancient Maya were very peaceful. Today, however,

   there is evidence that they _____ as peacefully as people
   (may / live)

   used to believe.

8. Burn marks on buildings, war images on buildings and pottery, and the discovery of weapons

   have led archaeologists to believe the Maya _____ in wars.
   (must / fight)

9. Archaeologist Arthur Demarest believes that after the year 751, there was intense rivalry

   among Mayan rulers. He says, "Their ferocious competition, which exploded into civil war,

   _____ what finally triggered the society's breakdown."
   (may / be)

10. The rain forests _____ enough food to support the Maya.
    (might / produce)

    Archaeologists have found evidence that at some point the rain forests were almost destroyed.

11. The Maya _____ to other areas in search of food. That
    (could / go)

    would explain their suddenly abandoning their homes.

12. The Maya _____ enough water. There was a four-month
    (might / have)

    dry period every year.

13. Some areas _____ from overpopulation. Archaeologist
    (may / suffer)

    T. Patrick Culbert estimates that there were as many as 200 people per square kilometer.

14. Overpopulation _____ to hunger. Human bones show
    (could / lead)

    evidence of poor nutrition.

15. Toward the end of their civilization, the Maya had so many problems that even a small

    disaster _____ them.
    (might / destroy)

16. Culbert says the final cause of destruction " _____
                                                    (could / be)

    something totally trivial—two bad hurricane seasons . . . or a crazy king."

3 | SHORT ANSWERS

*Some tourists in Central America are talking. Complete their conversations with the correct
form of the verbs in parentheses or with short answers.*

1. **A:** Those pyramids we saw were fascinating. Do you think they took a long time to build?

   B: _____*They must have*_____. According to our guide, the Maya didn't have
                  (must)

       horses or any other animals to carry the stone.

2. **A:** It was really hot out there today. Do you think it was more than 90 degrees?

   B: _____. Everyone was sweating.
              (must)

3. **A:** The tour guide was really informative. Do you think he's studied archaeology?

   B: _____. He surely knows a lot.
              (might)

4. **A:** I wonder if the guide ever heard of von Däniken's theories.

   B: _____. Von Däniken is pretty well known.
              (may)

5. **A:** I just called Sue's room, and there was no answer. Do you suppose she went out?

   B: _____. She said something about wanting to buy
              (could)

       some postcards.

6. **A:** Do you think *pok-a-tok* was a rough sport?

   B: _____. The players used to wear thick, heavy padding
   (must)

   for protection.

7. **A:** What did you think of lunch?

   B: It was very good. Did the Maya eat tortillas too?

   A: _____. Their main crop was corn, and archaeologists
   (must)

   have found *metates* in the ruins.

   B: *Metates*? What are those?

   A: Stones used for grinding corn into flour.

8. **A:** The guide didn't say anything about the tip we gave him. Do you think he was happy with it?

   B: _____. Maybe we didn't give him enough.
   (might not)

9. **A:** I don't feel well.

   B: Do you think it was something you ate?

   A: _____. We ate the exact same thing, and you're fine!
   (could not)

The Passive: Overview

1 | ACTIVE AND PASSIVE

*Write active and passive sentences. Use **they** in active sentences when you don't know the subject.*

1. (active)   They print the paper daily.

   (passive) *The paper is printed daily.*

2. (active)   *The political editor discovered a serious mistake.*

   (passive) A serious mistake was discovered by the political editor.

3. (active)   They fired several employees as a result of the mistake.

   (passive) _____

4. (active)   They published an article about China last month.

   (passive) _____

5. (active) _____

   (passive) The article was written by Al Baker.

6. (active) _____

   (passive) New editors are frequently hired at the newspaper.

7. (active)   Two of the new editors interviewed Marla Jacobson.

   (passive) _____

8. (active) _____

   (passive) Marla was given an assignment on the Philippines.

9. (active)   Marla researched the article thoroughly.

   (passive) _____

10. (active) _____

    (passive) Our readers were fascinated by the information.

2 | PASSIVE STATEMENTS: SIMPLE PRESENT AND SIMPLE PAST

Complete the facts about the Philippines with the passive form of the verbs in parentheses.

1. The Philippines _____ *were named* _____ by the Spanish explorer Villalobos in 1543.
    (name)

2. The islands _____ Filipinas to honor the Prince of Asturias, who later
    (call)
   became King Phillip II of Spain.

3. Today, the country _____ officially as the Republic of the Philippines.
    (know)

4. The nation _____ of 7,100 islands.
    (make up)

5. Only 11 of them _____ major islands.
    (consider)

6. An old legend says that the Philippines _____ when a giant threw a
    (form)
   huge mass of rock into the sea.

7. Many of the tiny islands _____ names.
    (not give)

8. The largest island _____ Luzon.
    (call)

9. The second-largest island _____ Mindanao.
    (name)

3 | ACTIVE OR PASSIVE

Here are some more facts about the Philippines. Complete the sentences with the active or passive form of the verbs in parentheses.

1. The Philippines _____ *are located* _____ in the tropics.
    (locate)

2. Most people _____ *live* _____ in the lowlands.
    (live)

3. Even the mountains _____.
    (inhabit)

4. Large rivers _____ on the main islands.
    (find)

5. Floods often _____ roads and bridges.
    (damage)

6. Windstorms _____ property damage and loss of life.
    (cause)

7. Long ago, most of the land _____ by forests.
    (cover)

8. Today, forests _____ over 70,000 square miles.
    (cover)

9. They _____ more than 3,000 kinds of trees.
    (contain)

10. Wild hogs _____ on most of the islands.
                  (find)

11. Water buffalos _____ for cultivating the flooded rice fields.
                  (use)

12. About 1,000 species of birds and 2,000 species of fish _____ the
                                                     (inhabit)

    Philippines.

4 | THE PASSIVE: WITH OR WITHOUT AN AGENT

Complete the information about the Philippines. Use the passive form of the verbs in the first set of parentheses. Include the agent in the second set of parentheses only when necessary.

1. When the Spanish explorers came to the Philippines in the 1500s, the islands

   _____ *were inhabited by three groups of people* _____.
                     (inhabit) (three groups of people)

2. The Aëtas _____ *are believed* _____ to be the earliest inhabitants.
                      (believe) (people)

3. Thousands of years later, the Aëtas _____.
                                   (follow) (groups from Indonesia)

4. Today, 8 native languages and almost 90 dialects _____
                                        (speak) (the Filipinos)

   in the Philippines.

5. Because they are similar, most dialects _____.
                                    (understand) (speakers of other dialects)

6. On December 31, 1937, Tagalog _____
                                    (declare) (President Manuel Quezon)

   to be the official language of the Philippines.

7. Today it _____.
                          (speak) (more than 70 million people)

8. Tagalog _____ in schools throughout the Philippines.
                   (teach) (teachers)

9. Tagalog belongs to the Austronesian family of languages, which _____
                                        (speak) (people)

   all across the Pacific, from Hawaii to Taiwan.

10. English _____ for commercial and business purposes.
                     (use) (people)

5 | QUESTIONS AND SHORT ANSWERS

Look at this map of Bolivia.

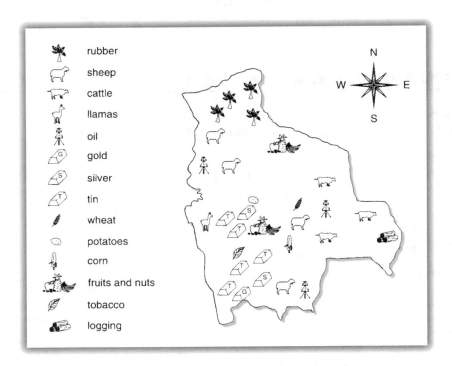

*Now write questions with the passive form of the words. Use the information in the map to answer the questions. Write short answers to **yes/no** questions and complete sentences for **wh-** questions.*

1. tin / mine / in the north?

   A: _Is tin mined in the north?_____

   B: _No, it isn't._____

2. What other minerals / mine in Bolivia?

   A: _What other minerals are mined in Bolivia?_____

   B: _Gold and silver are mined in Bolivia._____

3. Where / fruits and nuts / grow?

   A: _____

   B: _____

4. Where / logging / do?

   A: _____

   B: _____

5. What animals / raise?

    A: _____

    B: _____

6. llamas / find / in the east?

    A: _____

    B: _____

7. potatoes / grow?

    A: _____

    B: _____

8. Where / rubber / produce?

    A: _____

    B: _____

9. Where / oil / find?

    A: _____

    B: _____

10. wheat / grow / in the north?

    A: _____

    B: _____

11. cattle / raise / in the east?

    A: _____

    B: _____

UNIT 19 The Passive with Modals and Similar Expressions

1 | ACTIVE AND PASSIVE

*Write active and passive sentences. Use **they** in active sentences when you don't know the subject.*

1. (active)   *Many countries will build new airports soon.*

   (passive) New airports will be built by many countries soon.

2. (active)   They may construct some new airports on islands.

   (passive) _____

3. (active)   _____

   (passive) Passenger facilities might be put on decks under the runways.

4. (active)   They could save a lot of space that way.

   (passive) _____

5. (active)   _____

   (passive) An island airport had to be built in Osaka Bay by the Japanese.

6. (active)   At the old airport, they couldn't handle all the air traffic.

   (passive) _____

7. (active)   They had to move huge amounts of earth from nearby mountains.

   (passive) _____

8. (active)   Hong Kong's island airport will impress international visitors.

   (passive) _____

9. (active)   _____

   (passive) The airport can be reached easily by travelers.

10. (active) Before, they could reach Lantau only by ferry.

   (passive) _____

2 | AFFIRMATIVE AND NEGATIVE STATEMENTS

Complete this article with the correct form of the words in parentheses. Choose between affirmative and negative forms.

BRIDGING CULTURES
by Abdul Santana

While astronauts are working out cultural differences

on international space projects, people here on earth

_____*could be brought*_____ closer together than
1. **(could / bring)**

ever before. Engineers believe that many bodies of land,

including continents, _____ by bridges and tunnels. One of these
2. **(can / connect)**

ventures has already been completed. Some others _____ very soon
3. **(will / start)**

and _____ before too long. Here's a sample of places that
4. **(may / complete)**

_____ by these projects:
5. **(be going to / link)**

England and Europe. The Chunnel between France and England, the first of these projects,

has been operating since 1994. Passengers _____ now

_____ by train under the English Channel. Unfortunately for driving
6. **(can / carry)**

enthusiasts, individual cars _____ through the Chunnel. However, there
7. **(may / drive)**

is a shuttle, and in this way, up to 180 vehicles at a time _____.
8. **(are able to / transport)**

Asia and North America. According to engineer T.Y. Lin, small islands in the Bering Strait

_____ by a bridge carrying a railroad line, a highway, and oil and gas
9. **(could / join)**

pipelines. The bridge _____ the Intercontinental Peace Bridge.
10. **(will / call)**

(continued)

Africa and Europe. A new bridge connecting the continents of Europe and Africa

_____ probably _____ across the Strait of Gibraltar. More than nine
　　　　　　　　　　　　　　11. (will / build)

miles _____ by the structure. Obviously, new techniques
　　　　12. (must / bridge)

_____ because the bridge will be three times higher than any
　　　　13. (have to / develop)

bridge built so far.

Thailand, Malay Peninsula. In Southeast Asia, a new bridge called the Trans-Thai Landbridge

_____ from the Andaman Sea to the Gulf of Thailand. New ports and
　　　　14. (will / build)

towns _____ in this project.
　　　　15. (will / include)

Italy and Sicily. Every year, 14 million people cross the Strait of Messina between Sicily and

Italy. These travelers have been promised a bridge and highway for a long time, but this promise

_____ as quickly as people would like. Frequent earthquakes
　　　　16. (might / fulfill)

and dangerous winds of more than 125 mph mean that unfortunately some delays

_____. These problems _____, promise
　　　　17. (can / avoid)　　　　　　　　　　　　　　**18. (will / solve)**

engineers, who propose a two-mile extension bridge that can withstand both quakes and high

---

3 | QUESTIONS AND SHORT ANSWERS

Complete this interview between EuroTravel _magazine (EM) and Jean-Paul David (JD)._
Use the correct form of the words in parentheses or short answers where appropriate.

EM: I'd like to ask some questions about the Chunnel. First, _____can_____ vehicles

_____be driven_____ through it?
　　1. (can / drive)

JD: _____. Vehicles are carried on a special train called Le Shuttle.
　　　　　　2.

EM: _____ the cars _____ during the trip?
　　　　　　　　　　　　　　　　　3. (have to / occupy)

JD: _____. Drivers can get out and walk alongside their vehicles if
　　　　　　4.

they want.

EM: Now, what about the regular passenger train—the Eurostar? _____ tickets

_____ in advance?
    5. (Should / purchase)

JD: _____. In fact, not only do you need a ticket, but you also need to
            6.

check in at least 20 minutes before the train departs.

EM: At present, the Eurostar connects only a few cities. _____ service

_____ to include other cities?
    7. (be going to / expand)

JD: _____. There are plans to include many more cities. They are also
            8.

going to add European Night Service for passengers wishing to arrive in Paris or Brussels in

time for breakfast.

EM: _____ sleeping accommodations _____ for overnight
                                                        9. (Will / offer)

departures?

JD: _____. There will be both seated and sleeping accommodations.
            10.

EM: You mentioned breakfast. _____ food _____ aboard
                                                        11. (Can / purchase)

the Eurostar?

JD: _____. There are two buffet cars offering a large selection of hot
            12.

and cold food.

EM: Sounds good. Thanks. This information will be appreciated by our readers.

20 The Passive Causative

1 | PASSIVE CAUSATIVES

Rewrite the sentences using the passive causative.

1. Someone does my taxes every April.

   I have my taxes done every April.

2. Someone is repairing my computer.

   _____

3. My favorite mechanic at Majestic Motors checked my car.

   _____

4. Someone has just cleaned our windows.

   _____

5. Someone is going to cut our grass.

   _____

6. Someone must paint our house.

   _____

7. Someone should check our electrical wiring.

   _____

8. Northtown Contractors will probably do most of the work on our house.

   _____

9. They might build a new porch for us too.

   _____

10. Someone had better fix the neighbors' roof.

    _____

2 | **AFFIRMATIVE STATEMENTS**

Complete this article about consumer fraud. Use the passive causative of the verbs in parentheses.

Getting a Charge for Nothing

by Selma Johnson

After a disaster such as an earthquake or a flood, consumers should be prepared to protect themselves against dishonest businesses. As a result of damage to their homes, families must _____ *get* _____ major repairs _____ *done* _____. Working under great stress, they
1. (get / do)
sometimes _____ jobs _____ without getting estimates first. Often
2. (have / complete)
they _____ work _____ by dishonest electricians and other
3. (have / do)
contractors because they haven't checked with the Better Business Bureau first. The following is an example.

Following a major earthquake in Los Angeles, many people wanted to _____ their electric wiring systems _____. One electrician told a woman that she had to
4. (get / test)
_____ her circuit breakers _____ and charged her $510 per
5. (have / replace)
breaker. The same breakers cost just $21.86 apiece in a hardware store. *Dateline*, a television news show on NBC, decided to _____ the story _____. Using a
6. (have / investigate)
hidden camera, reporters and camera crews filmed the electrician's visit to another customer. This customer had a broken circuit breaker, so he _____ a new circuit breaker
_____ to replace it. But the electrician told him that he should also
7. (have / install)
_____ five other circuit breakers _____. And he charged $356 per
8. (get / replace)
breaker. Furthermore, the electrician said that if the customer _____ the job
_____ immediately, there was a risk of fire. *Dateline* _____ the
9. (not have / do)
"broken" circuit breakers _____. Not only did they not need replacement, but
10. (have / test)
the electrician went on to resell the "bad" breakers to other customers.

(continued)

Of course, the majority of workers are honest. But how can you, the consumer, guard against those who aren't? Here are some guidelines:

Be a smart consumer.

Do business only with service people who have good reputations. Before hiring unknown professionals, _____ them _____ by appropriate agencies to see
11. (have / check out)
that they are properly licensed. And although the Better Business Bureau will not make recommendations, they will tell you if they have received any complaints about a company.

Use a credit card if you can.

This way, if there is any problem, you will be able to _____ payment _____ until the issue is resolved. Your credit card company will even help you
12. (have / stop)
try to resolve the conflict.

Get an estimate.

Always try to get an estimate, and _____ it _____ in writing.
13. (have / put)

Know where to go for help.

If you think you have been a victim of fraud, notify your state Attorney General's Office. In many cities, newspaper and TV reporters also specialize in helping consumers. If they can't help, you will at least have the satisfaction of _____ the problem _____.
14. (get / publicize)

3 | *YES/NO* AND *WH-* QUESTIONS

Tyler is talking to his friend Frank about his car. Use the words in parentheses and the passive causative to write Frank's questions.

1. **FRANK:** My old Ford's been giving me trouble lately.

   Where do you usually get your car serviced?
   (Where / usually / get / your car / service)

   TYLER: I always go to Majestic Motors.

2. **FRANK:** _____
   (How often / get / it / do)

   TYLER: Oh, about every 5,000 miles. In fact, I was there just yesterday.

3. **FRANK:** Really? _____
   (get / it / winterize)

   TYLER: Well, they put antifreeze in the radiator.

4. **FRANK:** _____
   (ever / get / snow tires / put on)

   TYLER: No, I haven't. We really don't get enough snow around here for that. But we *are* going to take a trip to Canada this winter.

5. **FRANK:** _____
   (get / snow tires / put on / for the trip)

   TYLER: I guess it's not a bad idea.

6. **FRANK:** You bought your car in 2003. Right?

   _____
   (How many times / get / it / check / since then)

   TYLER: I can't say exactly. I do a lot of driving, so I've taken it in a lot.

7. **FRANK:** And you always go to Majestic for repairs and maintenance.

   _____
   (Why / get / the work / do / there)

   TYLER: The guy who owns it is a good mechanic, and I trust him. He'd never rip me off.

4 | AFFIRMATIVE AND NEGATIVE STATEMENTS

Frank took his car into Majestic Motors. Look at this portion of the checklist of services. Write all the things Frank had or didn't have done. Use the passive causative with **have** *or* **get**.

Majestic Motors

2680 Midlothian Tpke. (corner of Douglas Ave.) • Paramus, OH 45455 • (937) 555-3485

- -

[✓] check tire pressure   [ ] replace air filter

[ ] change oil   [ ] rotate tires

[ ] inspect undercarriage   [ ] adjust timing and engine speed

[✓] lubricate body and chassis   [✓] service automatic transmission

[✓] inspect air filter   [✓] flush cooling system

---

1. *He had the tire pressure checked.*

2. *He didn't have the oil changed.*

3. _____

4. _____

5. _____

6. _____

7. _____

8. _____

9. _____

10. _____

5 | EDITING

Read this e-mail. There are nine mistakes in the use of the passive causative. The first mistake is already corrected. Find and correct eight more.

Dear Petra,

    We've just ~~have~~ *had* our furniture brought over from the apartment, and we're really excited about moving into our "new" (but very old) house. A 19th-century millionaire had this place build for his daughter by a builder. We were able to afford it because it's a real "fixer-upper." It needs to has a lot of work done. We've already gotten the roof fix, but we're not having the outside painting until fall. After we get repaired the plumbing, we'll paint the inside ourselves (we can't paint over those big water stains until the plumbers finish their work). It sounds awful, but just wait until you see it. There's a fireplace in every bedroom—we're get the chimneys cleaned before winter. And the windows are huge. In fact, they're so large that we can't wash them ourselves, so yesterday we had done them professionally.

    As you can imagine, we've both been pretty busy, but we'd love to see you. Are you brave enough to visit us?

Love,

Britta and Klaus

UNIT

21 Present Real Conditionals

1 | SIMPLE PRESENT

*Look at this schedule of airplane fares. Then read the statements. For each statement, write **That's right** or **That's wrong**. If the statement is wrong, correct the underlined information.*

AIR ITALY ✈ SUPER BARGAIN AIRFARES	Destination: Rome			
GATEWAY	OFF SEASON*		PEAK**	
	Round Trip	One Way	Round Trip	One Way
New York	$645	$375	$769	$439
Boston	$645	$375	$769	$439
Philadelphia	$669	$389	$795	$449
Washington	$669	$389	$795	$449
Chicago	$709	$405	$829	$469
Cincinnati	$709	$405	$829	$469
Atlanta	$729	$419	$855	$479

*Off Season: 4/1–5/31 and 10/1–10/31; **Peak: 6/1–9/30

1. If you leave from New York in April, you pay $375 for a <u>round-trip</u> ticket.

   That's wrong. If you leave from New York in April, you pay $375 for a one-way ticket.

2. If you leave from Boston in June, you pay $439 for a <u>one-way</u> ticket.

   That's right.

3. You pay <u>more</u> if you leave from Chicago than if you leave from New York.

4. If you travel in September, your ticket costs <u>less</u> than if you travel in October.

5. If you fly in May, you pay <u>peak</u>-season rates.

_____

6. If you buy a one-way ticket, you pay <u>half</u> the cost of a round-trip ticket.

_____

7. If you fly round trip from <u>Atlanta</u> in October, the ticket price is $729.

_____

8. If you fly from Chicago, the fare is <u>the same as</u> from Cincinnati.

_____

9. If you leave from <u>Boston</u>, you pay the same fare as from Philadelphia.

_____

10. If you fly from Philadelphia, you pay a <u>higher</u> fare than from Chicago.

_____

2 | IMPERATIVES AND MODALS

Read these conversations about traveling to Italy. Write conditional sentences to summarize the travel agent's advice.

1. TOURIST: We're thinking of going to Italy.

    AGENT: You should book a flight now.

    SUMMARY: *If you're thinking of going to Italy, you should book a flight now.*
    Things get booked early in the summer.

2. TOURIST: We're flexible.

    AGENT: Don't go in the summer.

    SUMMARY: *If you're flexible, don't go in the summer.*
    It's very hot and crowded in the summer. Besides, the rates are higher.

3. TOURIST: We don't want to spend a lot of money getting around in Rome.

    AGENT: Take public transportation.

    SUMMARY: _____
    Taxis are expensive. You can get around fine with buses and trains.

(continued)

4. TOURIST: We don't like to book hotels in advance.

    AGENT: Go to one of the Rome Provincial Tourist Offices.

    SUMMARY: _____
    They can help you find a room.

5. TOURIST: We prefer small hotels.

    AGENT: Stay at *pensiones*.

    SUMMARY: _____
    They're usually more intimate and personal than hotels.

6. TOURIST: My husband is very interested in architecture.

    AGENT: You must visit the Palazzo Ducale in Venice.

    SUMMARY: _____
    It's a gorgeous building made of pink-and-white marble.

7. TOURIST: We love opera.

    AGENT: You should attend an open-air performance in Verona's Roman Arena.

    SUMMARY: _____
    It's just a short distance from Venice.

8. TOURIST: I'm interested in seeing ancient ruins.

    Agent: You might want to consider a side trip to Ostia Antica.

    SUMMARY: _____
    The ruins there are as interesting as the ones in Pompeii, and they're only a 30-minute train ride from Rome.

9. TOURIST: We plan to take a hair dryer and an electric shaver with us.

    AGENT: Don't forget to take a transformer and an adapter.

    SUMMARY: _____
    The electricity varies considerably in Italy, and unlike in the United States and Canada, outlets have round holes.

10. TOURIST: We want to have a really good dinner our first night there.

    AGENT: You should try Sabatini's.

    SUMMARY: _____
    It's one of the most popular restaurants in Rome. I hear that the spaghetti with seafood is excellent.

3 | SIMPLE PRESENT, IMPERATIVES, AND MODALS

*Complete this article about health advice for travelers. Combine the two sentences to make a real conditional sentence. Keep the same order and decide which clause begins with **if**. Make necessary changes in capitalization and punctuation.*

If You Go, Go Safely

It can happen. You're miles away from home on vacation or a business trip and you feel sick. What should you do? Here are some tips from travel experts.

1. (You travel. You need to take special health precautions.)

   If you travel, you need to take special health precautions.

   A little preplanning can go a long way in making your trip a healthier one.

2. (Don't pack medication in your luggage. You plan to check your luggage on the plane.)

   Don't pack medication in your luggage if you plan to check your luggage on the plane.

   Keep it in your carry-on bags. That way, if the airline loses your luggage, you won't be left without your medicine.

3. (You should bring along copies of your prescriptions. You take prescription medication.)

   _____

   _____

   Make sure they are written in the generic (not the brand-name) form.

4. (Notify the flight attendant or train conductor. You feel sick on board a plane or train.)

   _____

   _____

   They are trained to deal with the situation.

(*continued*)

5. (Call your own doctor. You are traveling in your own country when you feel sick.)

_____

_____

He or she may be able to refer you to a doctor in the area.

6. (Your hotel can recommend a doctor. You need medical attention in a foreign country.)

_____

_____

As an alternative, you can contact your embassy or consulate.

7. (You experience chest pains, weakness in an arm or leg, or shortness of breath. Get yourself to an emergency room.)

_____

_____

These can be symptoms of a heart attack. Time is of the utmost importance.

8. (You're not sure how serious your symptoms are. Assume they are serious and take appropriate steps.)

_____

_____

It's better to be safe than sorry. Many travelers tend to ignore symptoms when they are away from home.

9. (Don't drive to the hospital. You need to go to the emergency room.)

_____

_____

It's easy to get lost in an unfamiliar location. Take a taxi instead.

10. (You wear glasses. Take an extra pair with you.)

_____

_____

Many a vacation has been ruined by this lack of foresight.

Have a safe trip!

Future Real Conditionals

1 | IF AND *UNLESS*, AFFIRMATIVE AND NEGATIVE, SIMPLE PRESENT AND FUTURE

Circle the correct words to complete this Internet health and fitness quiz.
(Note: You can find the answers to the quiz in Exercise 3.)

HEALTH AND FITNESS QUIZ
Fact or Fiction?
How much do you really know about health and fitness?
Put your knowledge to the test.

	Fact	Fiction
1. **If** / Unless you want to be thin, you will have to watch your **a.** calorie intake.	○	○
2. If you <u>skip / will skip</u> a meal, you'll eat fewer calories each **b.** day, so you'll lose weight.	○	○
3. It will be difficult for you to lose weight and keep it off <u>if / unless</u> you <u>exercise / will exercise</u> regularly. **c.** **d.**	○	○
4. Carrots are good for your eyesight. <u>If / Unless</u> you eat **e.** them, your vision will improve.	○	○

5. If you <u>change / will change</u> your eating habits and become
    f.
a vegetarian, you <u>are / will be</u> healthier.
          g.
	○	○

(continued)

		Fact	Fiction

6. If you <u>take / will take</u> vitamin C daily, you <u>catch / won't catch</u>   ○   ○
        h.   **i.**
a cold.

7. If your body <u>has / will have</u> too much vitamin A, you might   ○   ○
                  j.
experience health problems.

8. You are <u>having / are going to have</u> trouble staying healthy   ○   ○
                k.
<u>if / unless</u> you drink eight glasses of water a day.
   l.

9. <u>If / Unless</u> you <u>go / will go</u> outside with wet hair when the   ○   ○
   m.   **n.**
weather is cold, you'll get sick.

SUBMIT

---

2 | CONDITIONAL QUESTIONS AND RESPONSES: AFFIRMATIVE AND NEGATIVE

Complete the conversation with the correct form of the words in parentheses or with short answers.

RAÚL: I'm shocked by the number of people who believe everything they read on the Internet.

They should realize that if they _____ *use* _____ the Web, they're going to see
                                1. (use)

a lot of information that may not be true.

YAN: What do you mean?

RAÚL: At the moment, there are millions of sites on the Internet and in the not-too-distant future

there are going to be lots more. Anyone can put up a website.

YAN: I've never really thought about it before, but you're right. I'll be doing a project for my

writing class soon. If I _____ to use the Internet for my research,
               2. (decide)

how _____ I _____ about the accuracy of
                            3. (know)

a website?

RAÚL: First of all, consider the source. In other words, if you _____ to the
                                  4. (go)

sites of well-respected organizations, they _____ probably

_____ reliable information.
      5. (have)

YAN: _____ I _____ figure out who a website

6. (be able to)

belongs to if I _____ somewhere on the site?

7. (look)

RAÚL: _____. Look for an "About us" link on the home page. Most

8.

websites, especially legitimate ones, will provide this kind of information, and unless you

_____ it, you _____ certain about a site's

9. (have)　　　　　　　　　　　　　　10. (not be)

reliability.

YAN: Is there anything else I should look for?

RAÚL: If a Web address _____ with ".edu" or ".org," you

11. (end)

_____ probably _____ good information

12. (find)

there.

YAN: If I _____ ".com" as part of the address,

13. (see)

_____ that _____ me anything?

14. (tell)

RAÚL: _____. A ".com" extension will usually be used by people or

15.

businesses selling a product. The information on these commercial sites can be useful, but

its purpose might be to sell rather than inform.

YAN: I understand. Now, what can you tell me about Internet hoaxes?

RAÚL: They're quite common. Unless you _____ the junk mail filter to

16. (set)

keep them out of your e-mail, you _____ one sometime soon.

17. (receive)

YAN: If one of these messages _____ in my e-mail,

18. (show up)

_____ it _____ difficult to recognize?

19. (be)

RAÚL: _____. An e-mail hoax will be easy for you to spot.

20.

YAN: How?

RAÚL: Most of them will make ridiculous claims. According to one hoax, if people

_____ their hair with certain kinds of shampoo, they

21. (wash)

_____ cancer. Hoaxes will also claim to be true, and they'll use lots

22. (get)

of capital letters and exclamation points.

(continued)

YAN: What if I reply to the senders and ask them to stop sending me messages?

RAÚL: If you _____ to be a smart computer user, you
                        23. (want)

_____ anything except delete all junk mail, including hoaxes,
        24. (not do)

immediately.

3 | SENTENCE COMBINING WITH *IF* AND *UNLESS*

Here are the answers to the Internet quiz in Exercise 1. How many questions did you answer correctly? Find out below.

*Use the words in parentheses and **if** or **unless** to write future real conditional sentences. Keep the same order as the items in parentheses, and decide where to put **if** or **unless**. Add punctuation where necessary.*

1. Statement 1 is fact.

   You will be able to control your weight more easily if you limit your calorie intake.
   (you / be able to control / your weight more easily) (you / limit / your calorie intake)
   There's a direct connection between your weight and how many calories there are in the food you eat.

2. Statement 2 is fiction.

   If you don't eat a meal, you'll be hungrier at your next meal.
   (you / not / eat / a meal) (you / be / hungrier at your next meal)
   Then you'll overeat, and this will cause you to gain rather than lose weight.

3. Statement 3 is fact.

   _____

   _____
   (you / have / trouble losing weight) (you / get / regular exercise)
   Physical exercise will burn calories and increase your metabolism, which will speed up weight loss and help you keep the pounds (or kilos) off.

4. Statement 4 is fiction.

   _____

   _____
   (you / receive / some health benefits) (you / eat / carrots)
   However, they won't improve poor eyesight.

5. Statement 5 is fiction.

   _____

   _____
   (you / stop eating meat) (you / need / something to replace it in your diet)
   Some vegetarians end up eating a lot of dairy products such as cheese or foods like rice and pasta that have too many calories.

6. Statement 6 is fiction.

_____

_____
(you / have a cold)   (vitamin C / help relieve the symptoms)

However, according to recent research, vitamin C can't prevent colds.

7. Statement 7 is fact.

_____

_____
(you / suffer / possible negative effects)   (your body / get / too much vitamin A)

Some doctors now believe that an excess of vitamin A can cause bones to weaken and break. It's a good idea to talk to your physician about any vitamin supplements that you plan to take.

8. Statement 8 is fiction.

_____

_____
(you / not / get sick)   (you / not / drink / exactly eight glasses of water a day)

Sure, your body needs plenty of water, but the specific amount varies from person to person. Besides, you can get water from other kinds of drinks and from the food that you eat.

9. Statement 9 is fiction.

_____

_____
(you / not / have a problem going out with wet hair)   (you / be / worried about feeling cold or looking less than perfect)

It's just a myth that you can get sick by going out in the cold when your hair is wet.

1 | CONDITIONALS: AFFIRMATIVE AND NEGATIVE

Complete this fairy tale. Use the correct form of the verbs in parentheses.

Stone Soup

𝒪nce upon a time, there were three soldiers.
They were on their way home from the wars,
and they were very hungry and very tired.

"I wish we _____*had*_____ something good to eat," said the first soldier.
1. (have)

"And I wish we _____ in a nice warm bed," said the second.
2. (can / sleep)

"I wish those things _____ possible," said the third. "But they are not. We must

march on until we reach home."

So on they marched. Suddenly they came to a village. The villagers saw them coming. They

knew that soldiers are always hungry. But the villagers didn't have much food. They worried that

if they _____ food to the soldiers, then they themselves _____
     4. (offer)   **5. (not eat)**

that night. So they decided to hide all their food.

The three soldiers went to the first house. "Could you give us something to eat and a place to

sleep?"

"We _____ glad to give you food if we _____ any. But we
     6. (be)   **7. (have)**

don't. And we _____ gladly _____ you space to sleep if we
                                     8. (give)

_____ all of it ourselves. But all our beds are full."
     9. (not need)

And so it went with all the villagers. Everyone had a good excuse.

"We gave all our food to the soldiers who came before you."

"Our father's sick. We _____ you food if he _____ sick."
            10. (offer)   **11. (not be)**

"The harvest was bad, and we need the grain for cattle feed. If we _____ the
                                           12. (not need)

grain, we _____ it with you."
     13. (share)

The soldiers thought, and then they said, "We wish you _____ us something to
                                           14. (can / offer)

eat, but since you can't—well, we'll have to make stone soup."

"Stone soup?" The villagers had never heard of it before.

"First, we'll need a large pot," said the soldiers.

That was no problem. The villagers brought them the largest pot they could find.

"Now we need water to fill it and a fire to cook with."

The villagers brought buckets of water and built a fire in the village square.

"Now we need three round, smooth stones."

That, too, was no problem at all. The villagers brought them, and the soldiers dropped them

into the pot.

The soldiers stirred the pot and added some salt and pepper (all good soups have salt and

pepper).

(continued)

"Stones like these usually make a very fine soup, but if we _____ some carrots,
15. (have)

it _____ a lot better," they said.
16. (taste)

"I think I can find a carrot!" said one of the villagers. She ran home and got all the carrots she

had hidden from the soldiers.

"This soup _____ so much better if we _____ some cabbage in
17. (taste)   18. (put)

it," said the soldiers as they sliced the carrots. "We wish you _____ some cabbage.
19. (have)

It's a shame that you don't."

"Let me see if I can find one," said another villager. She went home and came back with three

cabbages that she had hidden from the soldiers.

"If we _____ a little beef and a few potatoes, this soup _____
20. (add)   21. (be)

good enough for a rich man's table."

No sooner said than done. The villagers ran to get the hidden food.

Just imagine! A rich man's soup—and all from just a few stones!

The soldiers continued cooking and sighed, "If we _____ in a little barley and a
22. (stir)

cup of milk, this soup _____ fit for the king himself."
23. (be)

The villagers were really impressed. The soldiers knew the king! They wished that *they*

_____ the king!
24. (know)

The villagers brought their hidden barley and milk to the soldiers, who stirred the ingredients

into the pot.

Finally the soup was ready. Tables were set up in the square, and torches were lit. The soup was

delicious. Fit for a king. But the villagers said to themselves, "If a king _____ this
25. (eat)

soup, he _____ bread, and a roast, and some cider to go with it, wouldn't he?"
26. (require)

Before not too long, everyone sat down to enjoy a great feast of roast, bread, cider, and soup.

Never before had they tasted such delicious soup. And imagine—

it was made just from stones!

2 | *WISH*: AFFIRMATIVE AND NEGATIVE STATEMENTS

Read these complaints by the villagers in the "Stone Soup" story. Rewrite the complaints as wishes.

1. We don't have enough food.

   We wish we had enough food.

2. The soldiers will keep asking for our food.

   _____

3. We have to hide our food from them.

   _____

4. We need all our grain to feed the cows.

   _____

5. All our beds are full.

   _____

6. There isn't enough room for the soldiers.

   _____

7. The king won't come here to eat with us.

   _____

8. We don't have a larger soup pot.

   _____

9. We can't have stone soup every day.

   _____

3 | CONDITIONALS: AFFIRMATIVE AND NEGATIVE

Rewrite these excuses, using the present and future unreal conditional.

1. We don't have food. That's why we can't feed the soldiers.

   If we had food, we could feed the soldiers.

2. I don't have potatoes. That's why I'm not going to make potato soup.

   _____

(continued)

3. My apartment is small. That's why I won't invite people over.

_____

4. Steak is expensive. That's why we don't eat it.

_____

5. My daughter is sick. That's why I won't go shopping later today.

_____

6. I have bad eyesight. That's why I can't join the army.

_____

7. The soup doesn't have seasoning in it. That's why it tastes so bland.

_____

8. I always hide my money. That's why I'm not able to find it now.

_____

9. I'm not rich. That's why I don't take vacations.

_____

10. I don't have the recipe. That's why I don't make stone soup.

_____

4 | GIVING ADVICE WITH *IF I WERE YOU...*

*Complete the conversations. Use **were** and the correct form of the verbs in parentheses to write present and future unreal conditionals giving advice.*

1. **A:** I don't know how to cook.

   B: *If I were you, I'd learn how to cook.*_____

   　　　　　　　　　　　　　　　　　　　　　(learn)

   It's an important skill to have.

2. **A:** I've never read a fairy tale.

   B: _____

   　　　　　　　　　　　　　　　　　　　　　(read)

   They're a lot of fun.

3. **A:** I've never tried cabbage soup.

   B: _____

   　　　　　　　　　　　　　　　　　　　　　(try)

   It's delicious, and it's healthy.

4. A: This soup tastes bland. Where's the salt?

   B: _____
                                                  (not add)

      Put some pepper in, instead.

5. A: I'm going to ask for a raise.

   B: _____
                                                  (not ask)

      You've only worked there a month.

6. A: *Rambo VI* is playing at the Cineplex. My daughter loves going to the movies.

   B: _____
                                                  (not take)

      It's very violent.

7. A: My landlord just raised the rent again.

   B: _____
                                                  (move)

      You can find a nice apartment for much less.

8. A: I'm exhausted, and I have no idea what to make for dinner.

   B: _____
                                                  (eat out)

      The place across the street has good food, and it's not expensive.

5 | YES / NO AND WH- QUESTIONS

Several scouts are sitting around a campfire. Write their questions using the present and future unreal conditional.

1. What / we / do / if / we / can't find the way back?

   What would we do if we couldn't find the way back?

2. Who / look for us / if / we / get lost?

   _____

3. Where / we / go / if / it / start to rain?

   _____

4. you / be afraid / if / we / see a bear?

   _____

(continued)

5. If / you / hear a loud growl / you / be scared?

_____

6. What / you / do / if / you / be in my place?

_____

7. What / we / do / if / we / run out of food?

_____

8. If / we / not have any more food / we / make stone soup?

_____

6 | EDITING

Read this scout's journal entry. There are nine mistakes in the use of present and future unreal conditionals. The first mistake is already corrected. Find and correct eight more.

> 11:00 P.M., June 11
> Somewhere in the forest
>
> _were_
> It's 11:00 P.M. and I'm still awake. I wish I ~~was~~ home. If I would be home, I would be asleep
> by now! But here I am in the middle of nowhere. My sleeping bag is really uncomfortable. If
> I were more comfortable, I will be able to sleep. What do my friends think if they could see
> me now?
>
> I'm cold, tired, and hungry. I wish I have something to eat. But all the food is locked up in
> the van, and everyone else is sound asleep. If I would have a book, I would read, but I
> didn't bring any books. Tonight, as we sat around the campfire, someone read a story
> called "Stone Soup." I'm so hungry that even stone soup sounds good to me. If I know the
> recipe, I made it.
>
> Well, I'm getting tired of holding this flashlight (I wish I would have a regular lamp!), so I
> think I'll try to fall asleep.

Past Unreal Conditionals

UNIT 24

1 | AFFIRMATIVE AND NEGATIVE STATEMENTS

Complete this article about Walt Disney with the correct form of the verbs in parentheses.

Walt Disney had a difficult childhood, but he transformed his hardships into magic. Looking back, one can see the seeds of Disney's imagination in those early experiences. It's even possible that Disney ___wouldn't have created___ his many magical worlds
1. (not create)
if his early years _____ happier.
2. (be)

Disney's father, Elias Disney, had had dreams too, but they never came true. After a business failure in Chicago, the Disneys moved to a farm in Missouri. If his two oldest brothers _____ farmwork more
3. (find)
enjoyable, Walt Disney's childhood _____ easier. However, the
4. (might / be)
oldest brothers soon returned to Chicago, and six-year-old Walt and his brother Roy were left to do the farm chores. Like the witch in *Snow White*, the Disneys sold apples door to door when they needed money. In time, Roy found jobs off the farm. Walt

_____ never _____ a carnival or
5. (see)
_____ a toy if Roy _____ extra cash.
6. (own)   **7. (not earn)**

Once, when Walt was seven, he painted large animals on the walls of the farmhouse. His father punished him severely, but others encouraged his talent. Some people believe that if the local physician, "Doc" Sherwood, _____ him a quarter for his
8. (not pay)

119

drawing of Doc's horse, Rupert, or if his Aunt Margaret _____ him a gift
9. (not give)

of drawing paper and crayons, Disney's genius _____ Elias's harsh
10. (not survive)

treatment.

In 1910, when Walt was nine, Elias sold the farm and bought a newspaper route in Kansas

City, Missouri. For six years, Walt started work at 3:30 every morning. He sometimes fell

asleep in the warm halls of apartment buildings or dozed over a toy on a family's porch while

he was delivering newspapers. If he _____ more sleep during this
11. (get)

period, he _____ more attention to his lessons. But under the
12. (can / pay)

circumstances, he didn't have much success at school.

If he _____ Walter Pfeiffer, Disney's Kansas City boyhood
13. (not meet)

_____ completely joyless. Pfeiffer's family enjoyed singing and telling
14. (might / be)

jokes, and they introduced Walt to vaudeville theater. "The Two Walts" even put together their

own show when they were 13. Disney's strict parents _____ if they
15. (disapprove)

_____ Walt was acting in vaudeville, so Walt used to sneak out
16. (know)

through his bedroom window to go to the theater to perform.

When Disney was 14, his father gave him permission to attend Saturday classes at the Kansas

City Art Institute. If Elias _____, Walt _____
17. (not agree)   18. (take)

longer to find his vocation, but he was already dreaming of becoming a cartoonist. He

overcame great obstacles in his career, but once he had studied at the Institute, he never lost his

determination to make his imagined worlds real.

2 | PAST CONDITIONAL WITH *WISH*

One of Disney's most popular movies was Mary Poppins.
Based on a book by P. L. Travers, the movie tells the story
of a wonderful nanny who comes to take care of Jane and
Michael Banks. Rewrite the sentences with **wish**.

1. MRS. BANKS: Our old nanny, Katie, left. She didn't give me any warning.

   I wish our old nanny, Katie, hadn't left.

   I wish she had given me some warning.

2. MR. AND MRS. BANKS: Mary Poppins, the new nanny, demanded two days off a month. She was so stubborn about it.

   _____

   _____

3. BERT THE MATCH-MAN (who drew pictures on the sidewalk for money): I didn't make any money from my pictures today. I couldn't take Mary Poppins out for tea.

   _____

   _____

4. JANE AND MICHAEL BANKS: Mary Poppins took her day off today. She went on a magical journey without us.

   _____

   _____

5. MICHAEL: I stole Mary Poppins's magic compass tonight. Those giant creatures from the four corners of the world frightened me.

   _____

   _____

6. THE BANKS FAMILY: Mary Poppins didn't want to stay forever. She left with the West Wind last night.

   _____

   _____

3 | AFFIRMATIVE AND NEGATIVE STATEMENTS

*Using the words in parentheses, combine each pair of sentences into one past unreal conditional sentence. Keep the same order and decide which clause begins with **if**. Make necessary changes in capitalization and punctuation.*

1. Disney lived on a farm. He drew wonderful cartoon animals. (might)

   If Disney hadn't lived on a farm, he might not have drawn wonderful cartoon animals.

   _____

2. He sold candy to train passengers as a boy. He loved model trains as an adult. (might)

   _____

   _____

3. He didn't join the army in World War I. He was too young. (would)

   _____

   _____

4. His friend Ub helped him buy a suit. Disney, who was shy, met his fiancée's parents. (could)

   _____

   _____

5. He didn't own the rights to his first cartoon characters. His distributor cheated him. (would)

   _____

   _____

6. His art lessons meant a lot to Disney. He paid for lessons for Disney Studio artists. (would)

   _____

   _____

7. A bank loaned Disney $1.5 million. He made *Snow White and the Seven Dwarfs*. (could)

   _____

   _____

8. The movie succeeded. The bank didn't take Disney's home, his studio, and the film. (would)

   _____

   _____

9. Disney died in 1966. He didn't see the opening of the EPCOT Center in Florida. (would)

_____

_____

10. He was a genius. He overcame his unhappy childhood. (might)

_____

_____

4 | QUESTIONS AND RESPONSES

Complete this article with the correct form of the verbs in parentheses or with short answers.

The Second Time Around . . .

Our readers have shared some problems and questions related to their first trip to Disney World. First-time visitors can use their experiences and have more fun the first time around.

★ Orlando

Q: We visited Disney World for the first time last April, during spring break. It was packed! I think we spent most of our time waiting in lines. Is it always like that? _____Would_____ we _____have avoided_____ crowds if we
                                                                 1. (avoid)
_____had visited_____ at another time? —**Fred and Betty Ruddle, Flint, Michigan**
        2. (visit)

A: _____Yes, you would have_____. Spring break is one of the most crowded times (along
                    3.
with the Christmas holiday season and Presidents' Day weekend). Next time, go between Thanksgiving and Christmas or between January 4 and the middle of February.

★ ★ ★ ★ ★

Q: We bought tickets to the park at our hotel (not a Disney hotel), and they were expensive. How much _____ we _____ if we
                                              4. (save)
_____ them at a Disney hotel? —**K. Lewis, Denver, Colorado**
   5. (buy)

A: Up to 10 percent at a Disney store or hotel. You can also save by buying in advance.

★ ★ ★ ★ ★

(continued)

Q: We visited Magic Kingdom first, and that was the end of the trip for our daughter—she never wanted to leave. She really couldn't appreciate EPCOT, which we visited next and which fascinated us. If you _____ the trip with a small child, where
6. (make)
_____ you _____ first? **—V. Luvik, Miami, Florida**
7. (go)

A: I suggest that families see EPCOT first, then MGM, and finally Magic Kingdom, which is fun for both adults and children.

★ ★ ★ ★ ★

Q: We stayed at a hotel inside the park because we wanted to be close to everything. It was very expensive, and we wonder if that was the right choice. _____ we _____ travel a long way to get to the park if we
8. (have to)
_____ inside the park? **—J. Méndez, San Juan, Puerto Rico**
9. (stay)

A: _____. In fact, some of the hotels outside the park are
10.
actually closer to Magic Kingdom than some hotels inside the park, and they can be from 40 to 60 percent cheaper.

★ ★ ★ ★ ★

Q: Our son was studying pirates at school, so our first day at Disney World we raced over to Pirates of the Caribbean. It was closed for repairs. If we _____
11. (call)
ahead, _____ they _____ us it was closed?
12. (tell)
—P. James, Syracuse, New York

A: _____. In fact, it's always a good idea to call and find
13.
out if any rides are closed.

★ ★ ★ ★ ★

Q: On our first trip, we were never sure what to do next, and we spent a lot of time just waiting. My husband blames the park, but I think it could have been fun. If we
_____ more, _____ we
14. (plan)
_____ our trip more? **—D. King, Dayton, Ohio**
15. (enjoy)

A: _____. There's so much to see that visitors can get
16.
overwhelmed. To get the best value for your money, plan each day ahead of time.

Direct and Indirect Speech

1 | DIRECT AND INDIRECT SPEECH

Circle the correct words to complete this article about lie-detector tests.

The Awful Truth

After the United States Supreme Court said / (told) employers that you / they were no

1.   **2.**

longer allowed to give lie-detector tests (also called polygraph tests) to people they wanted

to hire, I became curious about these tests. I talked to Erica Dale, who took one a couple of

years ago. She was one of the last employees in our organization to take the test.

"The examiner was very nice," she told me. "He asked her / me a lot of harmless

3.

questions at first." During the test, Erica told the examiner that I / she lived in the suburbs.

4.

When he asked, she said that it was / is Monday and that she took / had taken the bus to

5.   **6.**

my / her interview. Then he brought up some tougher subjects. "I told him / you that I

7.   **8.**

got / 'd gotten into trouble for stealing in high school," Erica said. "There wasn't any point

9.

in lying about it."

With its rows of knobs, its wires, and its coils of paper, a lie detector is definitely a low-

tech piece of equipment. The devices are still used by police even though experts say that

they didn't / don't measure truth—only physical reactions to questions. Some questions

10.

increase a person's blood pressure and create other physical changes that the polygraph

measures. "The tests are / were only about 50 percent accurate," says one critic. "They

11.

belong in museums."

(continued)

Buzz Faye, who served three years for a crime he didn't commit, agrees. After his arrest, officials gave him a lie-detector test. They told him that <u>we / they</u> <u>plan / planned</u> to drop

12.   13.
charges if <u>you / he</u> passed. "Hey, great," said Faye. Unfortunately, he failed—twice—and

14.
spent three years in jail. Later, someone <u>said / told</u> police that Faye

15.
<u>didn't commit / hadn't committed</u> the crime. Faye was released when the police learned the

16.
names of the real criminals.

A polygraph expert who saw the tests said that police <u>scored / had scored</u> Faye's tests

17.
improperly. Since his release, Faye has been campaigning against the use of polygraph tests.

2 | DIRECT AND INDIRECT SPEECH: NECESSARY AND OPTIONAL TENSE CHANGES

Complete the interviewer's report of this job applicant's statements during a lie-detector test. Change the verb tense for reported speech only when necessary.

The Applicant's Statements During the Test	The Interviewer's Report a Few Hours Later
1. "My name is Anita Bell."	She said *her name is Anita Bell.*
2. "It's Wednesday."	She said _____
3. "My husband drove me to the interview."	She stated _____
4. "Our house is near the lake."	She said _____
5. "I shoplifted a lipstick once as a teenager."	She admitted _____
6. "I went to my mother right away."	She added _____
7. "She took me to the store to return the lipstick."	She explained _____
8. "I always tell the truth."	She claimed _____
9. "The test seems easy."	She said _____
10. "I don't mind taking lie-detector tests."	She noted _____

3 | DIRECT AND INDIRECT SPEECH

Compare the statements below with the previous employer's information form. Use **say** *or* **tell** *to report the statements. Then write* **That's true** *or* **That's not true**.

BATES DEPARTMENT STORE
EMPLOYEE INFORMATION FORM

Name:	Ethan Taylor
Dates employed:	Feb. 2002–Jan. 2004
Position (start):	Salesclerk
Promotions?	No
How many employees did this employee supervise?	None
Salary:	Start: $20,500 per year Finish: $22,000
Supervisor's comments:	This employee performed well on the job. He was reliable, and he showed initiative in serving customers and keeping the department running smoothly.
Reason for leaving:	Laid off when the store reduced its staff
Eligible for rehire:	Yes

---

1. "My name is Ethan Taylor."

   He said his name is Ethan Taylor. That's true.

2. "I worked at Bates Department Store for four years."

   He told the interviewer that he'd worked at Bates Department Store for four years. That's not true.

3. "I was a salesclerk."

   _____

4. "Then I received a promotion to supervisor."

   _____

5. "I supervised five other salesclerks."

   _____

6. "I was a reliable employee."

   _____

(continued)

7. "I showed initiative."

_____

8. "My employers liked my work."

_____

9. "Bates didn't fire me."

_____

10. "I lost my job because of staff reductions."

_____

11. "I earned $25,000 a year."

_____

12. "I got a raise of more than $2,000."

_____

Indirect Speech: Tense Changes

1 | DIRECT AND INDIRECT SPEECH

In January 1994 there was a terrible earthquake in Los Angeles, California. Read what John Baker said about it in 1994. Then use **He said** *with indirect speech to write what a friend in New York reported a year later.*

1. "I am living in Los Angeles."

   He said that he was living in Los Angeles.

2. "I've been living here my whole life."

   _____

3. "I've experienced many earthquakes in my years here."

   _____

4. "This quake was the worst."

   _____

5. "I'll start to rebuild my home this week."

   _____

6. "I must make it stronger."

   _____

7. "I may get government aid next month."

   _____

8. "I can't afford earthquake insurance right now."

   _____

9. "I had looked into it before the earthquake."

   _____

10. "I should have bought some insurance then."

    _____

2 | DIRECT AND INDIRECT SPEECH

Read what people in Los Angeles said about the 1994 quake. Use **He said/She said** *to report the people's statements.*

1. "I was never so afraid in my life." —*Miriam Shakter, human resources manager*

   She said that she'd never been so afraid in her life.

2. "I felt a sensation of falling." —*Diane Stillman, paralegal*

3. "We were all pretty well prepared for an earthquake, but not for the fire."
   —*Al McNeill, Los Angeles resident*

4. "You can't save everyone." —*Orville Wright, firefighter*

5. "I haven't seen anything like it." —*Robert DeFeo, Chief of the Fire Department*

6. "It felt like a giant hand reaching down and shaking me." —*73-year-old man*

7. "I'm scared that there's going to be another one." —*eight-year-old girl*

8. "I'm so glad I'm here!" —*Andrea Donnellan, geophysicist*

9. "Although I've been through war in my country, I had no idea what to do in the quake."
   —*Nicaraguan woman*

10. "If they say my house can't be saved, I don't know what I'll do or where I'll go."
    —*Jill Banks-Barad, political consultant*

3 | INDIRECT STATEMENTS

Read this interview between Today's World (TW) *and geophysicist Dr. Ito.*

When the Earth Moves

An Interview with Geophysicist Melissa Ito

TW: *Was the Los Angeles quake the worst in California's history?*

ITO: Not at all. The San Francisco quake of 1906 was much worse.

TW: *Earthquakes aren't very common, are they?*

ITO: Actually, there could be as many as a million earthquakes a year.

TW: *A million a year!*

ITO: Yes. Several thousand of them may occur today. However, most will go unnoticed because they'll occur beneath the ocean surface.

TW: *But even those earthquakes can be dangerous.*

ITO: You're right. Some have started dangerous tidal waves. We all remember, for example, the terrible tsunami in December 2004 that occurred following an earthquake under the Indian Ocean. The tsunami killed hundreds of thousands of people.

TW: *What causes earthquakes?*

ITO: I can't explain in great detail because it would be too complicated. Basically, quakes happen as a result of sudden movement in the rocks below the earth's surface. Forces push against the rocks, and the rocks break along lines called *faults*. In fact, a hidden fault caused the January 1994 Los Angeles quake.

TW: *Southern California gets more than its fair share of quakes, doesn't it?*

ITO: Yes. It has had several strong quakes in the past 20 years.

TW: *Can't scientists predict them?*

ITO: Another interviewer asked me this same question yesterday. As I explained to him, scientists may be able to make more accurate predictions sometime in the future. At present, they can tell you where an earthquake will occur, but not when.

TW: *That's terrible. Isn't there anything we can do?*

ITO: Yes. Engineers have developed houses and other structures that are able to withstand earthquake shocks. Governments must enforce building requirements in earthquake zones to limit damage from earthquakes.

TW: *What can individual citizens do?*

ITO: People living in earthquake zones should always be prepared because a quake might occur at any time. It's a good idea for them to have an emergency plan and emergency equipment such as a first-aid kit, a battery-powered radio, a flashlight, and extra batteries.

(continued)

*Now read the following statements. For each statement, write **That's right** or*
That's wrong *and use the verb in parentheses to report what Dr. Ito said.*

1. The 1994 Los Angeles quake wasn't as bad as the quake that hit San Francisco in 1906.

   (said) *That's right. She said that the San Francisco quake of 1906 had been much worse.*

   _____

2. Earthquakes aren't common.

   (explain) *That's wrong. She explained that there could be as many as a million earthquakes a year.*

   _____

3. It's possible that there were earthquakes on the day of Dr. Ito's interview.

   (say) _____

   _____

4. Most quakes take place under water.

   (say) _____

   _____

5. Earthquakes beneath the ocean are not dangerous.

   (acknowledge) _____

   _____

6. There were a lot of people who died in the 2004 tsunami in the Indian Ocean.

   (add) _____

   _____

7. It's easy to explain the cause of earthquakes.

   (state) _____

   _____

8. A visible fault caused the 1994 Los Angeles quake.

   (indicate) _____

   _____

9. Southern California gets a lot of quakes.

   (note) _____

   _____

10. Another interviewer wanted to know about scientists' ability to predict earthquakes.

    (say) _____

    _____

11. Scientists will never be able to predict earthquakes accurately.

    (claim) _____

    _____

12. People living in earthquake zones can do something to be prepared.

    (say _____

    _____

1 | DIRECT AND INDIRECT SPEECH

Write sentences in direct and indirect speech. Choose between **She told me** *and* **She asked me** *for the sentences in indirect speech.*

1. (direct speech)   "Turn left."

   (indirect speech)   *She told me to turn left.*

2. (direct speech)   "Don't turn right."

   (indirect speech)   _____

3. (direct speech)   _____

   (indirect speech)   She told me to slow down.

4. (direct speech)   _____

   (indirect speech)   She told me not to drive so fast.

5. (direct speech)   "Can you please turn on the radio?"

   (indirect speech)   _____

6. (direct speech)   _____

   (indirect speech)   She asked me to open the window.

7. (direct speech)   _____

   (indirect speech)   She asked me to come in for coffee.

8. (direct speech)   "Don't park in the bus stop."

   (indirect speech)   _____

2 | **AFFIRMATIVE AND NEGATIVE COMMANDS**

Read the travel tips about the common and very dangerous problem of feeling sleepy when driving.

Tips for Staying Awake While Driving

1. Get enough sleep before beginning a long trip.
2. Eat something before leaving on a trip.
3. Don't rely on caffeinated beverages such as coffee or cola to stay awake.
4. Share the driving responsibilities with another person if possible.
5. Don't wait until you're sleepy to take a break.
6. Stop every couple of hours and stretch your legs by walking around.
7. Listen to music or a book on tape.
8. Don't daydream.
9. Don't park on the side of the road if you need to stop for a short nap.

Now complete the sentences, rewriting the advice in indirect speech.

1. IndependentTraveler.com tells *drivers to get enough sleep before beginning a long trip.*

2. The website tells *drivers to eat something before leaving on a trip.*

3. It also warns _____

4. The site tells _____

5. It tells _____

6. It urges _____

7. It advises _____

8. It cautions _____

9. It tells _____

3 | INDIRECT SPEECH

Circle the correct words to complete this journal entry.

Last Friday my neighbor called me. She (invited) / told me to go
1.
for a ride in her new car. I told her I would love to. As soon as I

got into the car, she told / invited me to buckle my seat belt. I was
2.
pleased because I thought this meant she was a safe driver. Was I

in for a surprise! I watched in dismay as the speedometer

approached and then passed 70 mph. I told her slow / to slow
3.
down. I begged her not to / to not speed.
4.

She slowed down for a while, but then she sped up again.

Suddenly we heard a siren. The police officer told us pull / to pull
5.
over and stop. He got out of the car and asked her

to show / not to show him her license. She only had a learner's
6.
permit! He advised / ordered her to give him the permit, and, after
7.
checking my license, he told me that to take / to take the wheel and
8.
follow him to the police station. Two hours later, on the way home

from the station, my neighbor invited / ordered me to have dinner
9.
at her place. She had just bought a new microwave oven that she

wanted to try out. I thanked her but asked her waiting / to wait
10.
until another day. I had a headache and needed to take a nap!

4 | DIRECT SPEECH

Reread the story in Exercise 3. Then rewrite the indirect speech as direct speech. The numbers in the art match the numbers in Exercise 3.

1. Would you like to go for a ride in my new car?

2. _____

3. _____

4. _____

5. _____

6. _____

7. _____

8. _____

9. _____

10. _____

Indirect Questions

1 | WORD ORDER

Lydia Chan interviewed her grandmother for a family-history project at school. The next day, her grandmother told a friend about their talk. Use the words in parentheses and write Lydia's questions as her grandmother reported them.

1. "Can I talk to you about your life?"

   She asked if she could talk to me about my life.
   _____
   (about my life / if / could / she / talk to me)

2. "Do you have time today?"

   _____
   (whether / had / I / time / yesterday)

3. "Could you show me some photos?"

   _____
   (could / I / if / show her some photos)

4. "What's your full name?"

   _____
   (was / my full name / what)

5. "Who chose your name?"

   _____
   (who / my name / had chosen)

6. "When were you born?"

   _____
   (born / I / when / was)

7. "What country did your family come from?"

   _____
   (my family / what country / had come from)

8. "Where were you born?"

_____

(where / I / born / was)

9. "What was your biggest adventure?"

_____

(my biggest adventure / had been / what)

10. "What are you most proud of?"

_____

(was / I / what / most proud of)

2 | CHANGES IN INDIRECT QUESTIONS

Complete the article, changing the direct questions in parentheses to indirect questions.

BRINGING HISTORY HOME

by Monica Lubecki

A poor young man who had just arrived in the United States saw a fruit vendor on a New York street. He pointed at a piece of fruit and paid for it. But he didn't ask _____*what it was*_____. He bit into what he
1. (What is it?)
thought was an orange and quickly spit it out. It was a bitter kumquat—and he had spent precious money on it!

The young man was my grandfather. My mother told the story countless times, always with the same sad little smile. I loved hearing it and interrupted with questions to prolong it. I always asked

_____. "Nineteen," she reported. Then I
2. (How old was he?)
asked _____. "Five cents." Finally, I
3. (How much did it cost?)
demanded to know _____. She always
4. (Why didn't he ask the name of the fruit?)
replied impatiently, "You know he couldn't speak English."

As an adult, I asked myself _____. Later,
5. (Why did the details seem so important?)
I learned that our story was a typical immigrant family story. Children in a new

(*continued*)

country couldn't ask _____, so the family
6. (How are we going to get by?)

told a story that explained the methods they used to survive. (Our family's rule
was "Ask questions!")

Everyone has good stories, and collecting them is an interesting way for
younger family members to stay close to older relatives and learn the family's
culture. Recently, my son Mark interviewed his grandfather, my husband's
father. If you'd like to try this in your family, here are the steps Mark took to
make his grandfather feel at ease.

1. Mark asked him politely _____.
7. (Do you have some time to talk to me?)

2. He found a quiet room to talk in and then asked his grandfather

_____.
8. (Do you feel comfortable here?)

3. To get started, Mark talked about an event that the two of them had

shared. He asked his grandfather _____.
9. (Do you remember our trip to the circus?)

When the interview got under way, Mark wanted to know about the details of
his grandfather's childhood. He asked him _____
10. (What did you wear to school?)

and _____. In addition, he asked
11. (What did your mother cook?)

_____. Then, when Mark asked him
12. (What hobbies did you have?)

_____, he learned how his hobby, amateur
13. (What was your most important decision?)

radio, led to his job in communications. When he asked his grandfather

_____, he learned about his fascination
14. (What new invention do you like best?)

with computers.

In this interview, Mark discovered things that we, his parents, had never
known about our own parents' generation and ideas.

3 | INDIRECT QUESTIONS

A reporter interviewed Maya Angelou, an American poet who has led a very interesting life. Read the interviewer's notes and report which of his questions he asked and which ones he didn't ask.

1. when/born?	
2. who/gave the nickname Maya?	brother Bailey (called her "Mine")
3. where/grew up?	St. Louis and San Francisco
4. why/moved to San Francisco?	
5. what/studied?	dance and drama in a special high school
6. worked during high school?	yes—streetcar conductor, cook, singer, dancer
7. ever lived in another country?	yes—in Egypt—with husband, a lawyer from South Africa
8. speak other languages?	yes—fluent in French, Spanish, Italian, Arabic, and Fanti
9. why/name first book *I know Why the Caged Bird Sings*?	
10. why/started writing?	inspired by a speech by Dr. Martin Luther King
11. studied writing?	
12. where/like to write?	in a motel room near her home

1. He didn't ask her when she was born.

2. He asked her who had given her the nickname Maya.

3. _____

4. _____

5. _____

6. _____

7. _____

8. _____

9. _____

10. _____

11. _____

12. _____

UNIT 29 Embedded Questions

1 | EMBEDDED QUESTIONS: WORD ORDER AND PUNCTUATION

Complete the conversation by changing the direct questions in parentheses to embedded questions. Use correct punctuation.

A: Do you know _if there is anything good on TV?_
   1. (Is there anything good on TV?)

B: There's a soccer game on this evening that I want to watch.

A: I don't understand _____
   2. (Why do you enjoy watching sports all the time?)

B: Well, I want to know _____
   3. (How can you watch those boring travel shows?)

A: I like to find out _____
   4. (What are the most popular travel destinations?)

B: But you never go anywhere. Can you remember _____
   5. (When was your last vacation?)

A: That's beside the point. I'm not sure _____
   But I can dream, can't I?   **6. (Am I going to take a vacation anytime soon?)**

B: OK. Can you explain _____
   7. (How are you going to pay for your dream vacation?)

A: I'm trying to figure out _____
   8. (How much will a volunteer vacation cost?)

B: I've always wondered _____
   9. (Do people really take vacations where they have to work?)

A: Of course they do. Volunteer vacations are becoming more and more popular. They're a great way to travel. They're not too expensive, and they give people a chance to see the world and help others at the same time.

B: Do you know _____
   10. (Which organization has volunteer vacations in Africa?)

A: The one that I've heard the most about is Global Volunteers, but there are other groups that arrange trips too.

B: Could you tell me _____
   11. (Where should I go for more information?)

A: The Internet is a good place to go—or you could try watching a few travel shows with me!

2 | EMBEDDED QUESTIONS: WORD ORDER AND PUNCTUATION

Look at the list of questions that students in a listening-speaking class prepared for Jake Davis, a guest speaker who was invited to their class to talk about volunteer vacations.

Questions for Mr. Davis

~~Why do students take volunteer vacations?~~

What is the average cost of a volunteer vacation?

Who pays for the trip?

When do most students take volunteer vacations?

How long do the trips usually last?

Will I have any free time on a volunteer vacation?

How far in advance do I have to plan a volunteer vacation?

Do I have to be over 21 to go on a volunteer vacation?

Are most of the volunteer opportunities in the U.S.?

Should students on a volunteer vacation bring any extra money?

Now complete the conversation that took place during the students' question-and-answer session with Mr. Davis. Choose the appropriate question from the list, and change it to an embedded question. Use correct punctuation.

1. **KHADIJA:** I'm not sure *why students take volunteer vacations.*
   Isn't the whole point of a vacation to relax and have fun?

   MR. DAVIS: Many students like the idea of traveling and doing service work. They can do something useful while they're experiencing a different culture, learning new ideas, and, yes, even having fun.

2. **VICKY:** I'm only 18, so I'd like to know _____

   MR. DAVIS: There are volunteer vacations for people of all ages, but you may need your parents' permission for some of them since you're not 21.

(continued)

3.   **Jin Ho:** Can you tell me _____

    Mr. Davis: The individual traveler pays.

4.   **Nida:** Could you explain _____

    Mr. Davis: The cost depends on the location, the length, and the type of trip. The price can be anywhere from several hundred to several thousand dollars.

5.   **Machiko:** Do you know _____

    Mr. Davis: It's always a good idea to have money for emergencies or something that you really want to buy as a souvenir.

6.   **Bill:** I'd like to find out _____

    Mr. Davis: You'll spend most of your time on a volunteer project, but you'll still have a chance to meet the local people and have cultural experiences on your own.

7.   **Gosha:** Can you tell me _____

    Mr. Davis: The majority of the trips are from one to three weeks.

8.   **Khadija:** I'm wondering _____

    Mr. Davis: Some travel during the summer, but others do a volunteer vacation when they have a semester break.

9.   **Nida:** Do you know _____

    Mr. Davis: Some are in the U.S., but there are volunteer opportunities in countries all around the world.

10.   **Ke:** I have a travel brochure about volunteer vacations, but it doesn't say _____

_____

    Mr. Davis: I suggest making your travel plans as soon as possible. That way, you'll be sure to get the trip that you want.

3 | INFINITIVES AFTER QUESTION WORDS

Read the conversation about traveling. Then use the correct question word and the infinitive form of the appropriate verbs to complete the summaries.

1.   **Sylvia:** There are several airlines that fly from Chicago to Madrid. I have no idea which one I should take.

    SUMMARY: Sylvia is trying to figure out _which airline to take._ _____

2.   **ANNE:** Look for a nonstop flight and the lowest possible airfare.

         SYLVIA: Where?

         ANNE: I usually go to a website like Orbitz or Travelocity.

         SUMMARY: Sylvia isn't sure _____

3.   **SYLVIA:** OK. I'm thinking about renting a car. My question is how.

         ANNE: It's cheaper if you rent a car before you leave. You can do that on Orbitz or Travelocity too.

         SUMMARY: Sylvia and Anne are discussing _____

4.   **SYLVIA:** That was easy enough.

         ANNE: What are you going to do about rental car insurance?

         SYLVIA: Oh, you're right. I'd better talk to my agent.

         SUMMARY: Sylvia will ask her insurance agent _____

5.   **ANNE:** Do you speak Spanish?

         SYLVIA: A little, and I know where I can go for an inexpensive language course.

         SUMMARY: Sylvia has already found out _____

6.   **ANNE:** How long are you going to stay in Spain?

         SYLVIA: Maybe two weeks—or maybe longer.

         SUMMARY: Sylvia can't decide _____

7.   **ANNE:** What kind of clothes are you going to pack?

         SYLVIA: I've been thinking about that a lot.

         SUMMARY: Sylvia is wondering _____

8.   **ANNE:** Is there someone you can talk to about hotels and restaurants?

         SYLVIA: I can't think of anyone.

         SUMMARY: Sylvia doesn't know _____

4 | EDITING

Read this e-mail. There are six mistakes in the use of embedded questions. The first mistake is already corrected. Find and correct five more. Don't forget to check punctuation.

Dear Alicia,

    I don't know when ~~are you~~ *you are* leaving for your trip, but I decided to write anyway. How are you? Dan and I and the kids are all fine. Busy as usual. Tonight Dan and I got a babysitter and went to the movies (we hardly ever have the chance to go out alone). We saw a romantic comedy called <u>The Wedding Date</u>. I don't know is it playing near you, but I recommend it.

    I was thinking about the last time we were in San Francisco together. Can you remember where we ate. I know the restaurant was somewhere in Chinatown, but I can't remember what it was called.

    I've been wondering why I haven't heard from Wu-lan? Do you know where did he move? I'd like to write to him, but I don't know how to contact him.

    Well, the summer is almost here. Let us know when can you come for a visit. It would be great to see you again.

All my best,

Lily

Workbook Answer Key

In this answer key, where the contracted form is given, the full form is often also correct, and where the full form is given, the contracted form is often also correct.

UNIT 1 (pages 1–4)

1

2. ask, asking
3. buys, buying
4. come, comes
5. do, doing
6. eats, eating
7. employ, employs
8. fly, flies
9. forgets, forgetting
10. have, having
11. hurries, hurrying
12. lie, lies
13. opens, opening
14. rains, raining
15. reaches, reaching
16. say, saying
17. ties, tying
18. travel, travels

2

A. 2. Are . . . taking
   3. is studying
   4. 's
   5. remember
   6. look
B. 1. Do . . . know
   2. teaches
   3. 's working
   4. does . . . mean
   5. don't believe
C. 1. do . . . spell
   2. have
   3. looks
D. 1. are . . . sitting
   2. don't seem
   3. 'm trying
   4. doesn't like
   5. writes
   6. is
   7. 's beginning
E. 1. Do . . . want
   2. is studying
   3. does . . . do
   4. analyzes
   5. write
   6. sign

3

2. doesn't know
3. is focusing
4. is writing
5. looks
6. studies
7. believe
8. gives
9. are using OR use
10. does . . . hope OR is . . . hoping
11. look
12. tells
13. Does . . . lean
14. indicates
15. represents
16. is planning
17. doesn't leave
18. avoids
19. show
20. 's
21. is investigating
22. thinks
23. takes
24. warns
25. doesn't guarantee

4

Hi!

Well, I'm here at my new school, and ~~I'm~~ I
~~liking~~ *like* it very much. I'm ~~study~~ *studying* English this semester,
but the classes are really different from our English
classes in Korea. My teachers ~~doesn't~~ *don't* know how to
speak Korean, and my classmates ~~are coming~~ *come* from
countries all around the world, so we use English
all the time. That ~~is meaning~~ *means* that I'm getting a lot
of good practice these days.

Although I'm very happy, ~~I'm~~ I sometimes
~~having~~ *have* problems. ~~I'm not~~ *I don't* understand my
classmates' names because they don't look or
sound like Korean names. I always ask the same
questions: "What's your name?" and "How ^*do* you
spell it?" My teachers want me to call them by
their first names. It's difficult for me to treat my
teachers so informally, but I ^*'m* trying. Slowly but
surely, I'm getting accustomed to my life here.

I miss you a lot. ~~Your~~ *You're* still my favorite English
teacher.
Hye Lee

UNIT 2 (pages 5–8)

1

2. apply
3. was, were
4. became
5. carried
6. developed
7. eat
8. fell
9. feel
10. got
11. grew
12. lived
13. meet
14. pay
15. permitted
16. planned
17. send
18. slept

2. met
3. asked
4. Was
5. did . . . notice
6. Were . . . going
7. found
8. didn't fall
9. were working
10. met
11. hired
12. was trying
13. was
14. was feeling OR felt
15. was pretending OR pretended
16. thought
17. wanted
18. was working
19. came
20. didn't ask
21. solved
22. stopped
23. fell
24. were taking
25. met
26. became
27. was dating
28. didn't seem
29. heard
30. was whispering
31. got
32. told
33. wanted
34. changed
35. realized
36. didn't stop
37. broke up
38. asked
39. was moving
40. saw
41. was sitting
42. was trying
43. jumped
44. thought
45. didn't ask
46. was helping
47. seemed
48. saw
49. introduced
50. invited

3

December 16

I'm really glad that I ~~was deciding~~ *decided* to rent this apartment. I almost ~~wasn't~~ *didn't* move here because the rent is a little high, but I'm happy to be here. All the other apartments I looked at ~~were seeming~~ *seemed* so small, and the neighborhoods just weren't as beautiful as this one. And moving wasn't as bad as I feared. My original plan was to take a week off from work, but when Hakim ~~was offering~~ *offered* to help, I didn't need so much time. What a great brother! We ~~were moving~~ *moved* everything into the apartment in two days. The man next door was really nice to us. On the second day, he even helped Hakim with some of the heavy furniture. His name is Jared. I ~~don't~~ *didn't* even unpack the kitchen stuff last weekend because I was so tired. Last night I ~~walking~~ *walked* Mitzi for only two blocks. When I came back, Jared ~~stood~~ *was standing* downstairs. I think I made him nervous because he ~~was dropping~~ *dropped* his mail when he saw me.

I'd like to ask him over for coffee this weekend (in order to thank him), but everything is still in boxes. Maybe in a couple of weeks . . .

UNIT 3 (pages 9–14)

1

2. brought, brought
3. chose, chosen
4. delayed, delayed
5. felt, felt
6. found, found
7. finished, finished
8. got, gotten
9. graduated, graduated
10. hid, hidden
11. noticed, noticed
12. omitted, omitted
13. owned, owned
14. read, read
15. replied, replied
16. ripped, ripped
17. showed, shown
18. spoke, spoken

2

2. She graduated from college in 1999.
3. She's been reporting OR She's reported crime news since 2002.
4. Recently, she's been researching crime in schools.
5. She's been working on her master's degree since 2002.
6. Her father worked for the Broadfield Police Department for 20 years.
7. Simon Pohlig moved to Broadfield in 1997.
8. He's owned Sharney's Restaurant since 1999.
9. He coached basketball for the Boys and Girls Club for two years.
10. He's written two cookbooks for children.
11. He's been planning a local television show for several months.
12. The groom's mother has been serving OR has served as president of TLC Meals, Inc. for two years.

3

2. applied
3. has been working OR has worked
4. has written
5. found, was
6. has attended
7. began, received
8. went on
9. has taken
10. started
11. didn't get
12. decided
13. hasn't received
14. lived
15. has lived OR has been living
16. has recommended OR recommended

17. left
18. hasn't told
19. didn't slant
20. explained

4

My son and his girlfriend have ~~made~~ *been making* wedding plans for the past few months. At first I was delighted, but last week I ~~have heard~~ *heard* something that changed my feelings. It seems that our future daughter-in-law has ~~been deciding~~ *decided* to keep her own last name after the wedding. Her reasons: First, she doesn't want to "lose her identity." Her parents ~~have named~~ *named* her 31 years ago, and she ~~was~~ *has been* Donna Esposito since then. She sees no reason to change now. Second, she is a member of the Rockland Symphony Orchestra and she ~~performed~~ *has performed* OR *has been performing* with them for eight years. As a result, she ~~already became~~ *has already become* known professionally by her maiden name.

John, when I've ~~gotten~~ *got* married, I didn't think of keeping my maiden name. I ~~have felt~~ *felt* so proud when I became "Mrs. Smith." We named our son after my father, but our surname showed that we three were a family.

I've ~~been reading~~ *read* two articles about this trend, and I can now understand her decision to use her maiden name professionally. But I still can't understand why she wants to use it socially.

My husband and I ~~tried~~ *have tried* many times to hide our hurt feelings, but it's been getting harder. I want to tell her and my son what I think, but my husband says it's none of our business.

My son ~~didn't say~~ *hasn't said* anything so far, so we don't know how he feels. ~~Have we been making~~ *Have we made* the right choice by keeping quiet?

A Concerned Mother Who ~~Hasn't Been Saying~~ *Hasn't Said* One Word Yet

UNIT 4 (pages 15–23)

1

2. break, broken
3. cutting, cut
4. doing, done
5. entertaining, entertained
6. fight, fighting
7. forgiving, forgiven
8. leading, led
9. planning, planned
10. practicing, practiced
11. quitting, quit
12. seek, seeking
13. sink, sinking
14. stealing, stolen
15. sweeping, swept
16. swimming, swum
17. telling, told
18. withdraw, withdrawing

2

2. had . . . won
3. hadn't learned
4. hadn't brought
5. had found
6. had . . . established
7. had earned
8. had offered
9. had . . . written
10. had received
11. hadn't gotten
12. had met
13. had starred
14. had opened
15. had become
16. had finished

3

2. Had he flown; No, he hadn't.
3. Had he arrived; No, he hadn't.
4. Had he received; Yes, he had.
5. Had he met; Yes, he had.
6. Had he eaten; No, he hadn't.
7. Had he prepared; Yes, he had.

4

2. hadn't been doing
3. had been raining
4. had been eating
5. hadn't been drinking
6. had been crying
7. had been laughing
8. had been washing OR had been doing
9. had been listening
10. hadn't been paying

5

2. How long had he been living in Hollywood when he finally found an acting job?
3. Had he really been working as a cook in a fast-food restaurant when he became a successful actor?
4. Where had he been studying when he decided to enroll in classes at the Actors Studio Drama School?
5. Why had he been taking courses in accounting when he began his acting classes?

6. How long had he been thinking about working behind the cameras when he directed his first film?

7. Had he been looking for investors for a long time when he started his own production company?

6

2. had decided
3. had been swimming
4. had . . . lost
5. had had
6. had been searching
7. hadn't found
8. had been working
9. had been living
10. had appeared
11. had been making

7

2. Before she became a professional dancer, she had been studying at a business college.

3. She had been a dancer on the popular TV show *In Living Color* before she danced with Janet Jackson.

4. By the time she appeared in her first major film, she had been dancing professionally for several years.

5. When she starred in *Selena*, she had already finished the action film *Money Train*.

6. She had divorced her first husband by the time she started her singing career.

7. She had made several films before she got the name "J. Lo."

8. When she set a record for #1 movie and #1 album on the same weekend, she had been dating Sean "P. Diddy" Combs.

9. When she filmed *Maid in Manhattan*, she hadn't ended her relationship with her second husband yet.

10. By the time she fell in love with Ben Affleck, she had gotten married twice.

11. Their movie *Gigli* had failed at the box office by the time she called off her wedding to Ben Affleck.

12. She married actor and singer Marc Anthony after she had called off her wedding to Ben Affleck.

UNIT 5 (pages 24–28)

1

2. I'll come
3. Are you taking
4. I'll hand
5. It's going to fall
6. You're moving
7. Are you driving, We're flying
8. are you getting, We're going to take
9. I'll drive, we're going to have

2

2. will be living
3. are going to be parking
4. aren't going to be preparing
5. will be eating
6. won't be driving
7. will be walking
8. will be moving
9. will . . . be saving
10. aren't going to be buying
11. aren't going to be paying
12. won't be worrying
13. will be providing
14. are going to be attending
15. will be helping
16. (will be) providing
17. are going to be seeing

3

2. are you going to be using the lawn mower tomorrow? No, I'm not.
3. will we be getting new washers?
4. will you be going to the post office tomorrow? Yes, I will.
5. are you going to be making?
6. Will the entertainment committee be planning anything else in the near future? Yes, we will.
7. Are we going to be meeting then? No, we aren't.

4

2. will be meeting with . . . faxes reports
3. attends . . . will be having a phone conference with John Smith
4. has (OR eats) . . . will be having (OR eating) lunch with Jack Allen
5. will be billing clients . . . drafts
6. picks up . . . will be taking Saril to the dentist
7. will be shopping for . . . takes Dursan to the barber
8. pays . . . will be cutting the grass

5

 'm going
I ~~go~~ to Jack's with the kids in a few minutes.
 playing   *we*
We'll be ~~play~~ cards until 10:30 or so. While ~~we'll~~
play cards, Jack's daughter will be watching the
 's going to
kids. It ~~will~~ rain, so I closed all the windows. Don't
 starts OR *'s starting*   *'ll*
forget to watch "CSI"! It~~'ll start~~ at 10:00. I call
you after the card game because by the time we get
 'll be sleeping
home, you~~'re sleeping~~. Enjoy your evening.

UNIT 6 (pages 29–33)

1

2. will have completed
3. will have helped
4. 'll have been using OR 'll have used
5. 'll have bought
6. 'll have wrapped
7. won't have planned
8. won't have decided
9. 'll . . . have been arguing OR 'll . . . have argued
10. won't have wasted
11. 'll have completed
12. 'll have had
13. 'll have participated
14. (will have) redecorated
15. 'll have made
16. 'll have done
17. 'll have straightened
18. 'll have packed
19. 'll have been explaining

2

1. Yes, I will (have).
2. will you have been performing
3. will you have sewn
4. will the kids have been waiting OR will the kids have waited
5. will the paint have dried; No, it won't (have).
6. Will the cleaners have delivered; Yes, they will (have).
7. will we have been living OR will we have lived

3

2. A: How long will Aida have been walking by August 31?
   B: She'll have been walking (for) a month.
3. A: How many rooms will Arnie have painted by August 5?
   B: He'll have painted three rooms.
4. A: How long will Arnie have been painting downstairs by August 15?
   B: He'll have been painting downstairs (for) four days.
5. A: On August 16, will Arnie have left for his dentist appointment by 4:00?
   B: Yes, he will (have).
6. A: Will Aida have unpacked all the fall clothing by August 23?
   B: No, she won't (have).

7. A: How long will Aida have been driving in the carpool by August 19?
   B: She'll have been driving in the carpool (for) two weeks.
8. A: How many quarts of blueberries will Corrie have picked by August 19?
   B: She'll have picked three quarts of blueberries.
9. A: How many pies will Aida have baked by August 21?
   B: She'll have baked six pies.
10. A: Will they have finished packing for the trip by August 31?
    B: Yes, they will (have).

UNIT 7 (pages 34–38)

1

2. doesn't it?; No, it doesn't.
3. is it?; No, it isn't.
4. haven't you?; Yes, I have.
5. does it?; Yes, it does.
6. didn't you?; Yes, I did.
7. doesn't it?; Yes, it does.
8. can I?; Yes, you can.
9. will you?; No, I won't.
10. don't you?; Yes, I do.

2

2. Didn't Greenwood build a public beach? No, it didn't.
3. Isn't there an airport in Greenwood? No, there isn't.
4. Can't you see live theater performances in Greenwood? No, you can't.
5. Don't people in Greenwood shop at a nearby mall? Yes, they do.
6. Isn't the average rent in Greenwood under $700? Yes, it is.
7. Hasn't Greenwood been a town for more than a hundred years? Yes, it has.
8. Aren't they going to build a baseball stadium in Greenwood? Yes, they are.

3

A. 3. isn't it
B. 1. have you
   2. Didn't . . . fill out
   3. shouldn't we
C. 1. Isn't
   2. Didn't . . . use to be
   3. had it
D. 1. aren't they
   2. have you
   3. Can't . . . take

4

3. This is a good building, isn't it? OR Isn't this a good building?
4. The owner takes good care of it, doesn't he? OR Doesn't the owner take good care of it?
5. He's just finished renovations on the lobby, hasn't he? OR Hasn't he just finished renovations on the lobby?
6. He didn't paint our apartment before we moved in, did he?
7. He doesn't talk very much, does he?
8. The rent won't increase next year, will it?
9. Some new people will be moving into Apartment 1B, won't they? OR Won't some new people be moving into Apartment 1B?
10. This is a really nice place to live, isn't it? OR Isn't this a really nice place to live?

UNIT 8 (pages 39–42)

1

3. so	8. aren't
4. too	9. didn't
5. neither	10. and
6. had	11. too
7. but	

2

A. 2. didn't either
   3. am too
   4. did too
   5. so did
   6. but . . . don't
B. 1. but . . . didn't
   2. neither had
   3. so did
   4. but . . . wasn't
C. 1. are too
   2. so will

3

2. but Pleucadeuc wasn't
3. and neither does Beijing OR and Beijing doesn't either
4. but the Pleucadeuc and Beijing festivals are
5. and Pleucadeuc will too OR and so will Pleucadeuc
6. and so should participants at Pleucadeuc OR and participants at Pleucadeuc should too
7. and the Beijing festival doesn't either OR and neither does the Beijing festival
8. and so does Pleucadeuc OR and Pleucadeuc does too
9. but triplets, quads, and quints don't
10. and neither did Beijing OR and Beijing didn't either
11. and their families have too OR and so have their families

UNIT 9 (pages 43–49)

1

3. to watch	12. watching
4. to watch	13. watching
5. to watch	14. watching
6. to watch OR watching	15. to watch
7. to watch	16. watching
8. watching	17. watching
9. to watch	18. watching
10. watching	19. to watch
11. to watch OR watching	20. to watch

2

2. watching	18. not permitting
3. to recall	19. to watch
4. hearing	20. to understand
5. to calm	21. making
6. Sponsoring	22. to develop
7. to limit	23. (to) get rid of
8. to participate	24. to offer
9. creating	25. to advertise
10. to preview	26. to decrease
11. having	27. not to continue
12. to believe	28. to avoid OR avoiding
13. viewing	29. not to pay
14. interacting	30. to investigate
15. to behave	31. to schedule
16. to produce	32. turning on
17. limiting OR to limit	

3

2. unwilling to change
3. used to putting
4. fed up with seeing
5. likely to hit
6. force . . . to rate
7. hesitate to tell
8. decided to run
9. stopped showing
10. dislike turning off
11. insist on changing
12. forbid . . . to turn on
13. permit . . . to tune in
14. consider owning
15. advise . . . to do
16. keep communicating
17. hesitate to ask
18. agreeing to speak

2. A V-chip interferes with Annie's (OR Annie) watching violent shows.
3. *Reading Rainbow* encourages them to get interested in books.
4. Her father told Jennifer not to watch cop shows anymore.
5. The teacher recommended their watching *Nick News*.
6. Bob didn't (OR doesn't) remember their (OR them) seeing that game.
7. Sharif's parents persuaded him not to watch *Z-Men*.
8. The mother insisted on Sara's (OR Sara) turning off the TV.
9. Aziza wanted (OR wants) Ben to change the channel.
10. Nick can't get used to Paul's (OR Paul) watching a Spanish-language news program.

I'm tired of ~~hear~~ *hearing* that violence on TV causes violence at home, in school, and on the streets. Almost all young people watch TV, but not all of them are involved in committing crimes! In fact, very few people choose ~~acting~~ *to act* in violent ways. ~~To watch~~ *Watching* TV, therefore, is not the cause.

Groups like the American Medical Society should stop making a point of ~~to tell~~ *telling* people what to watch. If we want ~~living~~ *to live* in a free society, it is necessary ~~having~~ *to have* freedom of choice. Children need ~~learn~~ *to learn* values from their parents. It should be the parents' responsibility ~~deciding~~ *to decide* what their child can or cannot watch. The government and other interest groups should avoid ~~to interfere~~ *interfering* in these personal decisions. Limiting our freedom of choice is not the answer. If parents teach their children ~~respecting~~ *to respect* life, children can enjoy ~~to watch~~ *watching* TV without any negative effects.

UNIT 10 (pages 50–54)

2. let	5. make	8. help
3. help	6. get	9. gets
4. makes	7. have	10. let

11. makes 13. have
12. help 14. make

2. you keep
3. you (to) decide
4. them give
5. her to do
6. them take care of
7. them to realize
8. him to calm down
9. her play
10. him (to) adjust
11. him spend
12. him to obey
13. him understand
14. you (to) relax
15. us provide

2. got him to agree to adopt a dog or a cat.
3. let him make the choice.
4. made him do some research on pet care.
5. didn't help him do the research. OR didn't help him to do the research.
6. got her to fill out and sign the adoption application forms.
7. had him explain the adoption process (to her).
8. didn't make him pay the adoption fees.

Thanks for staying in touch. Your e-mails always make me ~~to smile~~ *smile*—even when I'm feeling stressed. Knowing that I have a good friend like you really helps me relax and not take things so seriously. My classes are difficult this semester. I still can't believe that three of my professors are making ~~them~~ *me* OR *us* write 20-page papers.

At the end of last semester, my roommates and I decided to get a dog. Actually, my roommates made the decision and then got me ~~go~~ *to go* along with it. I made them promise to take care of the dog, but guess who's doing most of the work! Don't misunderstand me. I love Ellie and appreciate what a great companion she is. I take her for a walk every morning and every night and ~~make~~ *let* her run and play in the park near our apartment as often as I can because I know how much she enjoys it. Still, I wish I could have my roommates ~~spend~~ *spend* just an hour a week with "our" dog. At this point, I can't even get them

to feed
~~feeding~~ Ellie, and now they want to move to an
apartment complex that won't let us ~~to have~~ a dog. *have*
I think I'm going to have to choose whether to live
with my roommates or with Ellie—and I think I'm
going to choose Ellie!
Take care. I'll write again soon.

UNIT 11 (pages 55–58)

1

2. up	10. out
3. over	11. up
4. ahead	12. down
5. out	13. up
6. down	14. down
7. over	15. off
8. out	16. up
9. back	

2

2. cut down	7. gets together
3. put together	8. give out
4. burns up	9. go out
5. sets up	10. go back
6. puts on	11. throws away

3

A. 2. pick them out
B. 1. empty out the money and everything else in
      your pockets
   2. throw it away
C. 1. set the firecrackers off
   2. keeps them away
D. 1. hanging these streamers up
   2. set it up
E. 1. write down all of the resolutions that I make
      each year
   2. gave them up

4

Wake ~~out~~ earlier. (No later than 7:30!) *up*
Work out at the gym at least 3 times a week.

Lose 5 pounds. (Give ~~over~~ eating so many *up*
desserts.)

Be more conscious of the environment:
   —Don't throw ~~down~~ newspapers. Recycle them. *away OR out*
   —Save energy. Turn ~~on~~ the lights when I leave *off OR out*
      the apartment.

Straighten up my room:
   —Hang ~~out~~ my clothes when I take ~~off them~~. *up* *them off*
   —Put my books back where they belong.
   —Give some of my old books and clothing that *away*
      I no longer wear ~~away~~.

Don't put off doing my homework assignments.
Hand ~~in them~~ on time! *them in*

Read more.

Use the dictionary more. (Look ~~over~~ words I don't *up*
know.)

When someone calls and leaves a message, call
them back right away. Don't put ~~off it~~! *it off*

Get to know my neighbors. Ask them for coffee *over*
~~over~~.

UNIT 12 (pages 59–63)

1

2. over	10. down
3. out	11. into
4. off	12. back
5. in (on) OR by	13. out
6. out	14. on
7. on	15. out
8. into	16. down
9. up	

2

A.		B.	
2. figured out		1. keep up with	
3. catch on		2. end up	
4. turning on		3. put . . . away	
5. teamed up with		4. use up	
6. help . . . out		5. found out	
7. go off		6. pick out	
8. takes away		7. look over	
9. turn . . . off		8. watch out for	

3

2. get along (well) with him
3. run into her
4. straighten it up
5. gotten together with them
6. pick them out OR pick some out
7. count on them
8. bring it out
9. picked it up
10. turn it down

11. cover them up
12. stuck to it
13. put them away
14. turn it on
15. figure it out

4

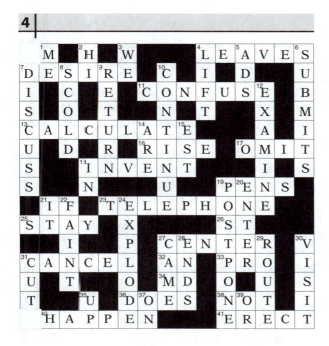

UNIT 13 (pages 64–67)

1

2. whose	**6.** that	**9.** who	**12.** who
3. who	**7.** whose	**10.** that	**13.** that
4. who	**8.** that	**11.** whose	**14.** who
5. that			

2

3. that OR which	**20.** makes
4. occur	**21.** that OR which
5. who OR that	**22.** holds
6. stay	**23.** that OR which
7. who OR that	**24.** surrounds
8. make	**25.** who OR that
9. that OR which	**26.** know
10. don't change	**27.** that OR which
11. that OR which	**28.** has
12. remain	**29.** who OR that
13. whose	**30.** has
14. come	**31.** whose
15. who OR that	**32.** are
16. are	**33.** who OR that
17. that OR which	**34.** consider
18. helps	**35.** who OR that
19. that OR which	**36.** seize

3

2. She was visiting her favorite aunt, whose apartment was right across from mine.

3. I was immediately attracted to Rebecca because of her smile, which was full of warmth and good humor.

4. I could see that Rebecca was a terrific woman whose interests were similar to mine. OR I could see that Rebecca was a terrific woman, whose interests were similar to mine.

5. Ballroom dancing, which was very popular in those days, was one of our favorite activities.

6. We also enjoyed playing cards with some of our close friends who (OR that) lived in the neighborhood.

7. Our friend Mike, who was a professional skier, taught us how to ski.

8. We got married in a ski lodge that (OR which) was in Vermont.

9. Our marriage, which means a lot to us both, has grown through the years.

10. The love and companionship that (OR which) make us very happy have gotten stronger.

11. Even the bad things that (OR which) have happened have brought us closer together.

12. I really love Rebecca, who is not only my wife but also my best friend.

UNIT 14 (pages 68–73)

1

A. 2. who	**F. 1.** that
B. 1. who	**2.** where
2. who	**3.** who
3. whom	**G. 1.** whose
C. 1. who	**2.** whose
2. who	**3.** who
3. whose	**4.** which
D. 1. who	**5.** who
2. where	**6.** whom
3. whom	
E. 1. which	
2. whose	
3. whom	
4. whose	
5. that	

2

2. where	**7.** writes
3. thanks	**8.** which OR that
4. whose	**9.** reads
5. finds, has found, OR found	**10.** which OR that
6. which OR that	**11.** face
	12. when OR that

13. runs out of OR
    has run out of
14. when
15. supported
16. which
17. praised
18. which
19. inserted
20. whom
21. feels
22. whom
23. dedicates OR
    has dedicated
24. where
25. has
26. which OR that
27. are supposed

Sentence 10: In her preface, Auel thanks a man she studied the art of making stone tools with.

Sentence 11: She also thanks an Arctic survival expert she met while she was doing research.

3

2. *The Clan of the Cave Bear*, which Auel started researching in 1977, tells the story of a clan of prehistoric people.
3. It took a lot of work to learn about these prehistoric people, whose lives Auel wanted to understand.
4. The clan lived during the Ice Age, when glaciers covered large parts of the earth.
5. The people lived near the shores of the Black Sea, where there are a lot of large caves.
6. The clan made their home in a large cave where bears had lived.
7. The task of hunting, which the men were responsible for, had great importance in the life of the Cave Bear Clan. OR The task of hunting, for which the men were responsible, had great importance in the life of the Cave Bear Clan.
8. One aspect of their lives which (OR that) Auel describes well was their technical skill.
9. She learned some of the arts that (OR which) prehistoric people had practiced.
10. In her preface, Auel thanks a man with whom she studied the art of making stone tools. OR Auel thanks a man who (OR whom) (OR that) she studied the art of making stone tools with.
11. She also thanks an Arctic survival expert who (OR whom) (OR that) she met while she was doing research.
12. He taught her to make a snow cave on Mt. Hood, where she spent one January night.
13. She went through a difficult time when she couldn't write.
14. A fiction writer whose lecture she attended inspired her to finish her book.
15. Jean Auel's novel, which she published in 1980, remains popular with fans around the world.

4

Sentence 8: One aspect of their lives Auel describes well was their technical skill.

Sentence 9: She learned some of the arts prehistoric people had practiced.

5

For my book report, I read *The Clan of the Cave Bear*, ~~that~~ *which* Jean M. Auel wrote after several years of research. In this novel about the life of prehistoric people, the main character is Ayla. She is found by a wandering clan after an earthquake kills her family. The same earthquake destroyed the cave in which this clan had lived, and they are searching for another home. The clan leader wants to leave Ayla to die. She is an Other—a human ~~which~~ *whose* language and culture his clan doesn't understand. However, the leader's sister Iza, *who* OR *whom* Ayla soon calls Mother, adopts her. ^

The story takes place at a time ~~where~~ *when* human beings are still evolving. Ayla is a new kind of human. Her brain, which she can use ✗ to predict and make plans, is different from Iza's and other clan members'. Their brains are adapted to memory, not new learning, ~~whom~~ *which* they fear and distrust. At first, Ayla brings luck to the clan. She accidentally wanders into a place where they find a large cave, perfect for their new home. She is educated by Iza, ~~who's~~ *whose* great knowledge everyone respects. The skills that Iza passes on to Ayla include healing and magic, as well as finding food, cooking, and sewing. However, Ayla's powers make it impossible for her to stay with the clan. She learns to hunt, a skill ~~where~~ *which* OR *that* OR (*pronoun deleted*) women are forbidden to practice. Her uncle, ~~that~~ *who* OR *whom* she loves very much, allows her to stay with the clan, but after he dies, she loses his protection. Another earthquake, for which she is blamed, destroys the clan's home, and she is forced to leave.

UNIT 15 (pages 74–77)

1

2. necessity
3. future possibility
4. assumption
5. assumption
6. necessity
7. prohibition
8. advice
9. future possibility
10. ability
11. prohibition

12. advice   14. ability
13. future possibility   15. advice

2

2. may not be
3. were able to fulfill
4. could catch
5. 'd better not jump
6. might see
7. can watch
8. may not sound
9. could harm
10. might shoot
11. doesn't have to use
12. 's able to catch
13. should take care of
14. might not mind

3

2. Should, 'd better not
3. 've got to, can
4. may not
5. must not, ought to
6. has to, should, may
7. 'd better not, weren't able to
8. could, must
9. 'd better, might not
10. can, were we able to
11. 've got to, don't have to
12. can't, should, have got to

4

    I have watched all of your shows several times, and I must ~~to be~~ *be* one of your biggest fans. The first time I saw you stick your hand in a nest of poisonous snakes, I ~~might not~~ *couldn't* believe my eyes. In fact, some people have come to the conclusion that you ~~ought to~~ *must OR have (got) to* be crazy to take risks like that. But they still ~~don't able to~~ *aren't able to OR can't* stop watching! Since your show started, you ~~can~~ *have been able to* make a lot of people interested in nature. I am one of those people.

    I am a high school senior, and because of your shows, I might major in zoology in college. I'm going to take general courses the first two years, so I ~~must not~~ *don't have to* choose my major yet. One of my concerns is that there ~~couldn't~~ *might not OR may not* be any jobs in zoology when I graduate. What is your opinion? Will there be a lot of jobs in this field in the next few years? My other problem is that my parents don't want me to work with animals. They haven't actually said, "You ~~don't have to~~ *must not OR can't* major in zoology," but they are very worried. What can I ~~to tell~~ *tell* them? I hope you will be able to find the time to answer this letter.

UNIT 16 (pages 78–81)

1

2. could . . . have done
3. Should . . . have let
4. Yes, you should have.
5. could have given
6. might have discussed
7. should . . . have handled
8. shouldn't have adjusted
9. ought to have faced
10. should have tried
11. Should . . . have ignored
12. No, you shouldn't have.
13. ought to have told
14. might have acted
15. Should . . . have complained
16. No, you shouldn't have.
17. ought to have been able to
18. shouldn't have spent
19. shouldn't have called
20. might have focused
21. could have admitted

2

2. They ought to have created a budget with some "personal money" for each partner.
3. He might have treated her attitude with respect.
4. She shouldn't have accused him of irresponsibility.
5. They should have planned ahead.
6. They could have scheduled time alone with each other.
7. He shouldn't have sulked.
8. They might have started with small tasks.
9. They could have provided containers to help organize the toys.
10. He shouldn't have given up and done it himself.

3

    I think my new roommate and I have both realized our mistakes. Reggie ~~should~~ *shouldn't* have demanded the biggest room in the apartment as soon as he arrived. He ought have *to* spoken to me first—after all, I've lived here ^ longer than he has. On the other hand, I really shouldn't ~~shout~~ *have shouted* at him as soon as he asked me. I could have ~~control~~ *controlled* my temper and just talked to him about the problem first. I felt really bad about that—until he invited friends over the night before I had to take a test!

Then I got so angry, I couldn't sleep. He might
have ~~asks~~ *asked* me first! I ~~oughta~~ *ought to* have said something
right away, but I didn't want to yell again. Of
course, some of my habits make Reggie mad too.
For example, I could've started washing my dishes
when he moved in, but I just let them pile up in the
sink. That was pretty gross—I definitely shouldn't
have ~~did~~ *done* that. But ~~should have he~~ *should he have* dumped all the
dirty dishes in my bedroom? He might ^*have* found a
better way to tell me he was annoyed. Last week,
he wanted to talk about our problems. As soon as
we started, I realized we should have talked much
sooner. Things have worked out a lot better since
our discussion.

UNIT 17 (pages 82–86)

1

2. couldn't have
3. must have
4. may have
5. must have
6. must have

7. could have
8. may have
9. could have
10. couldn't have
11. had to have

2

2. must not have been
3. had to have felt
4. must have occupied
5. may have traded
6. couldn't have lived
7. may not have lived
8. must have fought
9. may have been
10. might not have produced
11. could have gone
12. might not have had
13. may have suffered
14. could have led
15. might have destroyed
16. could have been

3

2. It must have been
3. He might have
4. He may have
5. She could have
6. It must have been
7. They must have
8. He might not have been
9. It couldn't have been

UNIT 18 (pages 87–91)

1

3. Several employees were fired as a result of the mistake.
4. An article about China was published last month.
5. Al Baker wrote the article.
6. They frequently hire new editors at the newspaper.
7. Marla Jacobson was interviewed by two of the new editors.
8. They gave Marla an assignment on the Philippines.
9. The article was researched thoroughly by Marla.
10. The information fascinated our readers.

2

2. were called
3. is known
4. is made up
5. are considered

6. were formed
7. were not given
8. is (OR was) called
9. is (OR was) named

3

3. are inhabited
4. are found
5. damage
6. cause
7. was covered

8. cover
9. contain
10. are found
11. are used
12. inhabit

4

3. were followed by groups from Indonesia
4. are spoken
5. are understood by speakers of other dialects
6. was declared by President Manuel Quezon
7. is spoken by more than 70 million people
8. is taught
9. are spoken (by people)
10. is used

5

3. Where are fruits and nuts grown? They're grown in the north (OR northeast) and in the central part of the country.
4. Where is logging done? It's done in the east.
5. What animals are raised? Sheep, cattle, and llamas are raised.
6. Are llamas found in the east? No, they aren't.
7. Are potatoes grown? Yes, they are.
8. Where is rubber produced? It's produced in the north.

9. Where is oil found? It's found in the south, east, and west (OR northwest).
10. Is wheat grown in the north? No, it isn't.
11. Are cattle raised in the east? Yes, they are.

UNIT 19 (pages 92–95)

1

2. Some new airports may be constructed on islands.
3. They might put passenger facilities on decks under the runways.
4. A lot of space could be saved that way.
5. The Japanese had to build an island airport in Osaka Bay.
6. At the old airport, all the air traffic couldn't be handled.
7. Huge amounts of earth had to be moved from nearby mountains.
8. International visitors will be impressed by Hong Kong's island airport.
9. Travelers can reach the airport easily.
10. Before, Lantau could be reached only by ferry.

2

2. can be connected
3. will be started
4. may be completed
5. are going to be linked
6. can . . . be carried
7. may not be driven
8. are able to be transported
9. could be joined
10. will be called
11. will . . . be built
12. must be bridged
13. have to be developed
14. will be built
15. will be included
16. might not be fulfilled
17. can't be avoided
18. will be solved

3

2. No, they can't
3. Do . . . have to be occupied
4. No, they don't
5. Should . . . be purchased
6. Yes, they should
7. Is . . . going to be expanded
8. Yes, it is
9. Will . . . be offered
10. Yes, they will

11. Can . . . be purchased
12. Yes, it can

UNIT 20 (pages 96–101)

1

2. I'm having (OR getting) my computer repaired.
3. I had (OR got) my car checked by my favorite mechanic at Majestic Motors.
4. We've just had (OR gotten) our windows cleaned.
5. We're going to have (OR get) our grass cut.
6. We must have (OR get) our house painted.
7. We should have (OR get) our electrical wiring checked.
8. We will probably have (OR get) most of the work on our house done by Northtown Contractors.
9. We might have (OR get) a new porch built (by them) too.
10. The neighbors had better have (OR get) their (OR the) roof fixed.

2

2. have . . . completed
3. have . . . done
4. get . . . tested
5. have . . . replaced
6. have . . . investigated
7. had . . . installed
8. get . . . replaced
9. didn't have . . . done
10. had . . . tested
11. have . . . checked out
12. have . . . stopped
13. have . . . put
14. getting . . . publicized

3

2. How often do you get it done?
3. Did you get it winterized?
4. Have you ever gotten snow tires put on?
5. Are you going to get (OR Will you get OR Are you getting) snow tires put on for the trip?
6. How many times have you gotten it checked since then?
7. Why do you get the work done there?

4

3. He didn't have (OR get) the undercarriage inspected.
4. He had (OR got) the body and chassis lubricated.

5. He had (OR got) the air filter inspected.
6. He didn't have (OR get) the air filter replaced.
7. He didn't have (OR get) the tires rotated.
8. He didn't have (OR get) the timing and engine speed adjusted.
9. He had (OR got) the automatic transmission serviced.
10. He had (OR got) the cooling system flushed.

5

We've just ~~have~~ *had* our furniture brought over from the apartment, and we're really excited about moving into our "new" (but very old) house. A 19th-century millionaire had this place ~~build~~ *built* for his daughter ~~by a builder~~. We were able to afford it because it's a real "fixer-upper." It needs to ~~has~~ *have* a lot of work done. We've already gotten the roof ~~fix~~ *fixed*, but we're not having the outside ~~painting~~ *painted* until fall. After we get ~~repaired the plumbing~~ *the plumbing repaired*, we'll paint the inside ourselves (we can't paint over those big water stains until the plumbers finish their work). It sounds awful, but just wait until you see it. There's a fireplace in every bedroom—we're ~~get~~ *getting* OR *going to get* the chimneys cleaned before winter. And the windows are huge. In fact, they're so large that we can't wash them ourselves, so yesterday we had ~~done them~~ *them done* professionally.

As you can imagine, we've both been pretty busy, but we'd love to see you. Are you brave enough to visit us?

UNIT 21 (pages 102–106)

1

3. That's right.
4. That's wrong. If you travel in September, your ticket costs more than if you travel in October.
5. That's wrong. If you fly in May, you pay off-season rates.
6. That's wrong. If you buy a one-way ticket, you pay more than half the cost of a round-trip ticket.
7. That's right.
8. That's right.
9. That's wrong. If you leave from Washington, you pay the same fare as from Philadelphia.
10. That's wrong. If you fly from Philadelphia, you pay a lower fare than from Chicago.

2

3. If you don't want to spend a lot of money getting around in Rome, take public transportation.
4. If you don't like to book hotels in advance, go to one of the Rome Provincial Tourist Offices.
5. If you prefer small hotels, stay at *pensiones*.
6. If your husband is very interested in architecture, you must visit the Palazzo Ducale in Venice.
7. If you love opera, you should attend an open-air performance in Verona's Roman Arena.
8. If you're interested in seeing ancient ruins, you might want to consider a side trip to Ostia Antica.
9. If you plan to take a hair dryer and an electric shaver with you, don't forget to take a transformer and an adapter.
10. If you want to have a really good dinner your first night there, you should try Sabatini's.

3

3. You should bring along copies of your prescriptions if you take prescription medication.
4. Notify the flight attendant or train conductor if you feel sick on board a plane or train.
5. Call your own doctor if you are traveling in your own country when you feel sick.
6. Your hotel can recommend a doctor if you need medical attention in a foreign country.
7. If you experience chest pains, weakness in an arm or leg, or shortness of breath, get yourself to an emergency room.
8. If you're not sure how serious your symptoms are, assume they are serious and take appropriate steps.
9. Don't drive to the hospital if you need to go to the emergency room.
10. If you wear glasses, take an extra pair with you.

UNIT 22 (pages 107–111)

1

b. skip
c. unless
d. exercise
e. If
f. change
g. will be
h. take
i. won't catch
j. has
k. are going to have
l. unless
m. If
n. go

2

2. decide
3. will . . . know OR am . . . going to know
4. go
5. 'll . . . have OR 're . . . going to have
6. Will . . . be able to OR Am . . . going to be able to
7. look
8. Yes, you will. OR Yes, you are.
9. have
10. won't be OR aren't going to be OR 're not going to be
11. ends
12. 'll . . . find OR 're . . . going to find
13. see
14. will . . . tell OR is . . . going to tell
15. Yes, it will. OR Yes, it is.
16. set
17. 'll receive OR 're going to receive
18. shows up
19. will . . . be OR is . . . going to be
20. No, it won't. OR No, it isn't.
21. wash
22. 'll get OR 're going to get
23. want
24. won't do OR 're not going to do OR aren't going to do

3

3. You'll have (OR You're going to have) trouble losing weight unless you get regular exercise.
4. You'll receive (OR You're going to receive) some health benefits if you eat carrots.
5. If you stop eating meat, you'll need (OR you're going to need) something to replace it in your diet.
6. If you have a cold, vitamin C will help (OR is going to help) relieve the symptoms.
7. You'll suffer (OR You're going to suffer) possible negative effects if your body gets too much vitamin A.
8. You won't get (OR You aren't going to get OR You're not going to get) sick if you don't drink exactly eight glasses of water a day.
9. You won't have (OR You aren't going to have OR You're not going to have) a problem going out with wet hair unless you're worried about feeling cold or looking less than perfect.

UNIT 23 (pages 112–118)

1

2. could sleep
3. were
4. offered
5. wouldn't eat

6. 'd be
7. had
8. 'd . . . give
9. didn't need
10. 'd offer
11. weren't
12. didn't need
13. 'd share
14. could offer
15. had
16. would taste
17. would taste
18. put
19. had
20. added
21. would be
22. stirred
23. would be
24. knew
25. ate
26. 'd require

2

2. We wish the soldiers wouldn't keep asking for our food.
3. We wish we didn't have to hide our food from them.
4. We wish we didn't need all our grain to feed the cows.
5. We wish all our beds weren't full.
6. We wish there were enough room for the soldiers.
7. We wish the king would come here to eat with us.
8. We wish we had a larger soup pot.
9. We wish we could have stone soup every day.

3

2. If I had potatoes, I'd make potato soup.
3. If my apartment weren't small, I'd invite people over.
4. If steak weren't expensive, we'd eat it.
5. If my daughter weren't sick, I'd go shopping later today.
6. If I didn't have bad eyesight, I could join the army.
7. If the soup had seasoning in it, it wouldn't taste so bland.
8. If I didn't always hide my money, I'd be able to find it now.
9. If I were rich, I'd take vacations.
10. If I had the recipe, I'd make stone soup.

4

2. If I were you, I'd read a fairy tale.
3. If I were you, I'd try cabbage soup.
4. If I were you, I wouldn't add salt.
5. If I were you, I wouldn't ask for a raise.
6. If I were you, I wouldn't take her to see *Rambo VI* (OR to that movie).
7. If I were you, I'd move.
8. If I were you, I'd eat out.

2. Who would look for us if we got lost?
3. Where would we go if it started to rain?
4. Would you be afraid if we saw a bear?
5. If you heard a loud growl, would you be scared?
6. What would you do if you were in my place?
7. What would we do if we ran out of food?
8. If we didn't have any more food, would we make stone soup?

It's 11:00 P.M. and I'm still awake. I wish I ~~was~~ *were* home. If I ~~would be~~ *were* home, I would be asleep by now! But here I am in the middle of nowhere. My sleeping bag is really uncomfortable. If I were more comfortable, I ~~will~~ *would* be able to sleep. What ~~do~~ *would* my friends think if they could see me now?

I'm cold, tired, and hungry. I wish I ~~have~~ *had* something to eat. But all the food is locked up in the van, and everyone else is sound asleep. If I ~~would have~~ *had* a book, I would read, but I didn't bring any books. Tonight, as we sat around the campfire, someone read a story called "Stone Soup." I'm so hungry that even stone soup sounds good to me. If I ~~know~~ *knew* the recipe, I ~~made~~ *would make* it.

Well, I'm getting tired of holding this flashlight (I wish I ~~would have~~ *had* a regular lamp!), so I think I'll try to fall asleep.

UNIT 24 (pages 119–124)

1

2. had been
3. had found
4. might have been
5. would . . . have seen
6. owned
7. hadn't earned
8. hadn't paid
9. hadn't given
10. wouldn't have survived
11. had gotten
12. could have paid
13. hadn't met
14. might have been
15. would have disapproved
16. had known
17. hadn't agreed
18. would have taken

2. We wish Mary Poppins, the new nanny, hadn't demanded two days off a month. We wish she hadn't been so stubborn about it.
3. I wish I had made (some) money from my pictures today. I wish I could have taken Mary Poppins out for tea.
4. We wish Mary Poppins hadn't taken her day off today. We wish she hadn't gone on a magical journey without us.
5. I wish I hadn't stolen Mary Poppins's magic compass tonight. I wish those giant creatures from the four corners of the world hadn't frightened me.
6. We wish Mary Poppins had wanted to stay forever. We wish she hadn't left with the West Wind last night.

2. If he hadn't sold candy to train passengers as a boy, he might not have loved model trains as an adult.
3. He would have joined the army in World War I if he hadn't been too young.
4. If his friend Ub hadn't helped him buy a suit, Disney, who was shy, couldn't have met his fiancée's parents.
5. If he had owned the rights to his first cartoon characters, his distributor wouldn't have cheated him.
6. If his art lessons hadn't meant a lot to Disney, he wouldn't have paid for lessons for Disney Studio artists.
7. If a bank hadn't loaned Disney $1.5 million, he couldn't have made *Snow White and the Seven Dwarfs*.
8. If the movie hadn't succeeded, the bank would have taken Disney's home, his studio, and the film.
9. If Disney hadn't died in 1966, he would have seen the opening of the EPCOT Center in Florida.
10. If he hadn't been a genius, he might not have overcome his unhappy childhood.

4. would . . . have saved
5. had bought
6. had made
7. would . . . have gone
8. Would . . . have had to
9. hadn't stayed
10. No, you wouldn't have.
11. had called

12. would . . . have told
13. Yes, they would have.
14. had planned
15. would . . . have enjoyed
16. Yes, you would have.

UNIT 25 (pages 125–128)

1

2. they
3. me
4. she
5. was
6. had taken
7. her
8. him
9. 'd gotten
10. don't
11. are
12. they
13. planned
14. he
15. told
16. hadn't committed
17. had scored

2

2. (that) it's Wednesday.
3. (that) her husband had driven her to the interview.
4. (that) their house is near the lake.
5. (that) she'd shoplifted a lipstick once as a teenager.
6. (that) she'd gone to her mother right away.
7. (that) she'd taken her to the store to return the lipstick.
8. (that) she always tells the truth.
9. (that) the test seems easy.
10. (that) she doesn't mind taking lie-detector tests.

3

3. He said (OR told the interviewer) (that) he'd been a salesclerk. That's true.
4. He said (OR told the interviewer) (that) he'd received a promotion to supervisor. That's not true.
5. He said (OR told the interviewer) (that) he'd supervised five other salesclerks. That's not true.
6. He said (OR told the interviewer) (that) he'd been a reliable employee. That's true.
7. He said (OR told the interviewer) (that) he'd shown initiative. That's true.
8. He said (OR told the interviewer) (that) his employers had liked his work. That's true.
9. He said (OR told the interviewer) (that) Bates hadn't fired him. That's true.
10. He said (OR told the interviewer) (that) he'd lost his job because of staff reductions. That's true.
11. He said (OR told the interviewer) (that) he'd earned $25,000 a year. That's not true.

12. He said (OR told the interviewer) (that) he'd gotten a raise of more than $2,000. That's not true.

UNIT 26 (pages 129–133)

1

2. He said (that) he'd been living there his whole life.
3. He said (that) he'd experienced many earthquakes in his years there.
4. He said (that) that quake had been the worst.
5. He said (that) he would start to rebuild his home that week.
6. He said (that) he had to make it stronger.
7. He said (that) he might get government aid the following month.
8. He said (that) he couldn't afford earthquake insurance right then.
9. He said (that) he had looked into it before the earthquake.
10. He said (that) he should have bought some insurance then.

2

2. She said (that) she'd felt a sensation of falling.
3. He said (that) they'd all been pretty well prepared for an earthquake, but not for the fire.
4. He said (that) you can't (OR couldn't) save everyone.
5. He said (that) he hadn't seen anything like it.
6. He said (that) it had felt like a giant hand reaching down and shaking him.
7. She said (that) she was scared that there was going to be another one.
8. She said (that) she was so glad she was there.
9. She said (that) although she'd been through war in her country, she'd had no idea what to do in the quake.
10. She said (that) if they said her house couldn't be saved, she didn't know what she'd do or where she'd go.

3

(*Answers may vary slightly.*)

3. That's right. She said (that) several thousand of them might occur that day.
4. That's right. She said (that) most would go unnoticed because they'd occur beneath the ocean surface.
5. That's wrong. She acknowledged (that) some had started dangerous tidal waves.

6. That's right. She added that the tsunami had killed hundreds of thousands of people.
7. That's wrong. She stated (that) she couldn't explain in great detail because it would be too complicated.
8. That's wrong. She indicated (that) a hidden fault had caused the 1994 Los Angeles quake.
9. That's right. She noted (that) it had had several strong quakes in the past 20 years.
10. That's right. She said (that) another interviewer had asked her that same question the day before.
11. That's wrong. She claimed (that) scientists might be able to make more accurate predictions sometime in the future.
12. That's right. She said (that) it was a good idea for them to have an emergency plan.

UNIT 27 (pages 134–137)

1

2. She told me not to turn right.
3. "Slow down."
4. "Don't drive so fast."
5. She asked me to turn on the radio.
6. "Can (OR Could) you please open the window?" OR "Please open the window."
7. "Please come in for coffee." OR "Come in for coffee, please." OR "Would you like to come in for coffee?"
8. She told me not to park in the bus stop.

2

3. drivers not to rely on caffeinated beverages such as coffee or cola to stay awake.
4. drivers to share the driving responsibilities with another person if possible.
5. drivers not to wait until they're sleepy to take a break.
6. drivers to stop every couple of hours and stretch their legs by walking around.
7. drivers to listen to music or a book on tape.
8. drivers not to daydream.
9. drivers not to park on the side of the road if they need to stop for a short nap.

3

2. told
3. to slow
4. not to
5. to pull
6. to show
7. ordered
8. to take
9. invited
10. to wait

4

2. (Please) buckle your seat belt.
3. (Please) slow down.
4. (Please) don't speed.
5. (Please) pull over and stop.
6. (Please) show me your license. OR Would you (please) show me your license?
7. (Please) give me the permit.
8. (Please) take the wheel (and follow me to the police station).
9. Would you like to have dinner at my place?
10. Could (OR Can) you wait until another day?

UNIT 28 (pages 138–141)

1

2. She asked (me) whether I had time yesterday.
3. She asked (me) if I could show her some photos.
4. She asked (me) what my full name was.
5. She asked (me) who had chosen my name.
6. She asked (me) when I was born.
7. She asked (me) what country my family had come from.
8. She asked (me) where I was born.
9. She asked (me) what my biggest adventure had been.
10. She asked (me) what I was most proud of.

2

2. how old he had been
3. how much it had cost
4. why he hadn't asked the name of the fruit
5. why the details had seemed so important
6. how they were going to get by
7. if (OR whether) he had some time to talk to him
8. if (OR whether) he felt comfortable there
9. if (OR whether) he remembered their trip to the circus
10. what he had worn to school
11. what his mother had cooked
12. what hobbies he had had
13. what his most important decision had been
14. what new invention he likes (OR liked) best

3

3. He asked her where she had grown up.
4. He didn't ask her why she had moved to San Francisco.
5. He asked her what she had studied.
6. He asked her if (OR whether) she had worked during high school.

7. He asked her if (OR whether) she had ever lived in another country.
8. He asked her if (OR whether) she speaks (OR spoke) other languages.
9. He didn't ask her why she had named her first book *I Know Why the Caged Bird Sings*.
10. He asked her why she had started writing.
11. He didn't ask her if (OR whether) she had studied writing.
12. He asked her where she likes (OR liked) to write.

UNIT 29 (pages 142–146)

1

2. why you enjoy watching sports all the time.
3. how you can watch those boring travel shows.
4. what the most popular travel destinations are.
5. when your last vacation was?
6. if (OR whether) I'm going to take a vacation anytime soon.
7. how you're going to pay for your dream vacation?
8. how much a volunteer vacation will cost.
9. if (OR whether) people really take vacations where they have to work.
10. which organization has volunteer vacations in Africa?
11. where I should go for more information?

2

2. if (OR whether) I have to be over 21 to go on a volunteer vacation.
3. who pays for the trip?
4. what the average cost of a volunteer vacation is?
5. if (OR whether) students on a volunteer vacation should bring any extra money?
6. if (OR whether) I'll have any free time on a volunteer vacation.
7. how long the trips usually last?
8. when most students take volunteer vacations.

9. if (OR whether) most of the volunteer opportunities are in the U.S.?
10. how far in advance I have to plan a volunteer vacation.

3

2. where to look for a nonstop flight and the lowest possible airfare.
3. how to rent a car.
4. what to do about rental car insurance.
5. where to go for an inexpensive language course.
6. how long to stay in Spain.
7. what kind of clothes to pack.
8. who to talk to about hotels and restaurants.

4

    I don't know when ~~are you~~ *you are* leaving for your trip, but I decided to write anyway. How are you? Dan and I and the kids are all fine. Busy as usual. Tonight Dan and I got a babysitter and went to the movies (we hardly ever have the chance to go out alone). We saw a romantic comedy called <u>The Wedding Date</u>. I don't know ~~is it~~ *if it's* playing near you, but I recommend it.

    I was thinking about the last time we were in San Francisco together. Can you remember where we ate*?* I know the restaurant was somewhere in Chinatown, but I can't remember what it was called.

    I've been wondering why I haven't heard from Wu-lan*.* Do you know where ~~did he move~~ *he moved*? I'd like to write to him, but I don't know how to contact him.

    Well, the summer is almost here. Let us know when ~~can you~~ *you can* come for a visit. It would be great to see you again.

Test: Units 1–4

PART ONE

Circle the letter of the correct answer to complete each sentence.

Example

Mark _____ a headache last night.   Ⓐ B C D

(A) had   (C) has had
(B) has   (D) was having

1. Water _____ at 0 degrees C.   A B C D

   (A) freezes   (C) has been freezing
   (B) froze   (D) is freezing

2. In our World History class, we _____ about the causes of the Korean War   A B C D
   this week.

   (A) learn   (C) are learning
   (B) was learning   (D) had learned

3. Sarah _____ glasses since she was a young girl. She can't see anything   A B C D
   without them.

   (A) wore   (C) is wearing
   (B) has worn   (D) wears

4. John _____. It really annoys me.   A B C D

   (A) always complain   (C) is always complaining
   (B) had always complained   (D) was always complaining

5. Vicki is planning to transfer to another school, but I _____ that she should   A B C D
   stay here.

   (A) thinking   (C) thought
   (B) 'd thought   (D) think

6. By 11:00 this morning, I _____ three cups of coffee.   A B C D

   (A) drink   (C) had drunk
   (B) had been drinking   (D) have drunk

7. I was listening to the radio when I _____ the news.   A B C D

   (A) hear   (C) 've heard
   (B) heard   (D) was hearing

(continued)

8. Ellen and Jack _____ in Europe when they met for the first time.   A B C D

   (A) traveled   (C) have been traveling
   (B) have traveled   (D) were traveling

9. We have been studying English grammar _____ six months.   A B C D

   (A) for   (C) already
   (B) since   (D) after

10. Can you please turn down the TV? The baby _____.   A B C D

   (A) has slept   (C) sleeps
   (B) is sleeping   (D) slept

11. The Morrisons _____ to Texas last September.   A B C D

   (A) had moved   (C) have moved
   (B) have been moving (D) moved

12. While Jedd was living in Toronto, Helen _____ in California.   A B C D

   (A) was living   (C) lives
   (B) had lived   (D) has lived

PART TWO

Each sentence has four underlined words or phrases. The four underlined parts of the sentence are marked A, B, C, and D. Circle the letter of the <u>one</u> underlined word or phrase that is NOT CORRECT.

Example
Rosa <u>rarely</u> <u>is using</u> public transportation, but <u>today</u> she <u>is taking</u> the bus.   A Ⓑ C D
     A   B   C   D

13. The doctor <u>called</u> <u>this morning</u> <u>while</u> you <u>slept</u>.   A B C D
          A   B   C   D

14. <u>When</u> the students <u>arrived</u>, their teacher <u>was giving</u> them an assignment   A B C D
    A   B   C
because they <u>needed</u> additional practice.
            D

15. I'm really hungry because I <u>haven't had</u> lunch <u>yet</u>, but I <u>wait</u> for my friends   A B C D
                         A   B   C
because I <u>want</u> to eat with them.
        D

16. <u>By the time</u> I <u>had gotten</u> home, the show <u>had</u> <u>already ended</u>.   A B C D
    A   B   C   D

17. Pete and Andy <u>were</u> <u>driving</u> to work <u>when</u> they <u>were seeing</u> the accident.   A B C D
            A   B   C   D

18. Erika <u>has</u> <u>been looking</u> for a job <u>since</u> she <u>has graduated</u> from college.   A B C D
       A   B   C   D

19. Janice didn't <u>own</u> a car then because she <u>hasn't</u> <u>learned</u> to drive <u>yet</u>.   A B C D
           A   B   C   D

20. I <u>had</u> <u>been living</u> in this apartment for ten years, but <u>I'm</u> <u>looking</u> for a new   A B C D
   A   B   C   D
one now.

Test: Units 5–6

PART ONE

Circle the letter of the correct answer to complete each sentence.

Example

Mark _____ a headache last night.   Ⓐ B C D

(A) had   (C) has had
(B) has   (D) was having

1. Bill will be _____ to Taipei tomorrow.   A B C D

(A) flies   (C) fly
(B) flying   (D) have been flying

2. We _____ a new TV soon.   A B C D

(A) own   (C) 're owning
(B) 'll own   (D) 'll have owned

3. Look at those dark clouds! It _____.   A B C D

(A) rains   (C) 's raining
(B) 's going to rain   (D) will rain

4. They'll be making photocopies while he _____ typing the report. A B C D

(A) finishes   (C) 'll finish
(B) 'l be finishing   (D) 's been finishing

5. I _____ be working tomorrow. I'll be out of town.   A B C D

(A) don't   (C) 'm not
(B) haven't   (D) won't

6. Kareem will _____ almost $1,000 by next year.   A B C D

(A) had saved   (C) have saved
(B) have been saving   (D) saves

7. We're late. When we _____ there, they'll already have eaten dinner. A B C D

(A) get   (C) 'll get
(B) got   (D) 'll have gotten

8. By the end of this week, Henry _____ regularly for six months. A B C D

(A) exercised   (C) will exercise
(B) exercises   (D) will have been exercising

(continued)

9. When I finish this story by Nguyen Treng, I'll _____ all of her mysteries.   A B C D

   (A) be reading   (C) have read
   (B) have been reading   (D) read

10. Next year, the Carters will have moved to their new house _____.   A B C D

   (A) already   (C) since
   (B) for   (D) yet

PART TWO

Each sentence has four underlined words or phrases. The four underlined parts of the sentence are marked A, B, C, and D. Circle the letter of the <u>one</u> underlined word or phrase that is NOT CORRECT.

Example
Rosa <u>rarely</u> <u>is using</u> public transportation, but <u>today</u> she <u>is taking</u> the bus.   A Ⓑ C D
    A   B   C   D

11. <u>Will</u> you <u>been</u> <u>going</u> to the supermarket <u>tonight</u>?   A B C D
    A   B C   D

12. <u>While</u> Bill <u>will wash</u> the dishes, <u>I'll</u> be <u>sweeping</u> the floor.   A B C D
    A   B   C   D

13. <u>By the time</u> I <u>got</u> home, <u>I'll have</u> <u>walked</u> three miles and I'll be ready for   A B C D
    A   B   C   D

   a big breakfast.

14. Professor Sanek <u>will have</u> <u>returned</u> to the office by 4:00, and he <u>calls</u>   A B C D
                    A   B   C

   you <u>then</u>.
       D

15. The Lees <u>will save</u> <u>for</u> ten years <u>by the time</u> their first child <u>enters</u> college.   A B C D
          A   B   C   D

16. Ana will <u>has</u> <u>been</u> watching TV <u>for</u> an hour by the time dinner <u>is</u> ready.   A B C D
             A   B   C   D

17. In the near future, most people in this country <u>will</u> <u>be</u> <u>work</u> in service jobs   A B C D
                                      A   B   C

   after they <u>complete</u> their education.
           D

18. At the end of this year, Tania <u>will</u> <u>be</u> free of debt because she will <u>already</u>   A B C D
                          A B   C

   have <u>been paying</u> her entire credit card bill.
       D

19. Tania <u>will</u> <u>have spent</u> $1,000 in interest <u>before</u> she <u>will pay off</u> her loan.   A B C D
        A   B   C   D

20. John loves that old suitcase. By the time he <u>gets</u> home from vacation   A B C D
                                  A

   <u>next month</u>, he'll <u>have</u> <u>carries</u> it at least 50,000 miles.
      B   C   D

Test: Units 7–8

Circle the letter of the correct answer to complete each sentence.

Example

Mark _____ a headache last night.

(A) had   (C) has had

(B) has   (D) was having

Ⓐ B C D

1. _____ you from Panama?

(A) Aren't   (C) Did

(B) Come   (D) Didn't

A B C D

2. Ben's not at work today, _____?

(A) does he   (C) is he

(B) doesn't he   (D) isn't he

A B C D

3. Your cousin lived in New York, _____?

(A) didn't she   (C) isn't she

(B) hadn't she   (D) wasn't she

A B C D

4. Miguel _____ here very long, has he?

(A) has been   (C) was

(B) hasn't been   (D) wasn't

A B C D

5. — Doesn't Sam own a house in Florida?
   — _____ He bought one there last year.

(A) No, he doesn't.   (C) Yes, he does.

(B) No, he didn't.   (D) Yes, he did.

A B C D

6. — Can't Rick speak Spanish?
   — _____ He never learned.

(A) No, he can't.   (C) Yes, he can.

(B) No, he doesn't.   (D) Yes, he does.

A B C D

(continued)

7. That's your notebook, isn't _____?　　　　　　　　　　　　A B C D

   (A) there　　　　　　　(C) yours
   (B) it　　　　　　　　 (D) that

8. — You're not Alex, are you?　　　　　　　　　　　　　　　A B C D
   — _____ I'm Alex Winslow.

   (A) No, I'm not.　　　　(C) Yes, I am.
   (B) No, you're not.　　 (D) Yes, you are.

9. — Today's July 5th, isn't it?　　　　　　　　　　　　　　A B C D
   — _____ It's the 6th.

   (A) Neither is it.　　　 (C) So is it.
   (B) No, it isn't.　　　　(D) Yes, it is.

10. They've read the paper, _____ I have too.　　　　　　　A B C D

   (A) and　　　　　　　　(C) either
   (B) but　　　　　　　　(D) neither

11. — Jennifer ate at home last night.　　　　　　　　　　　A B C D
    — _____ I saw him having dinner at Manny's Diner.

   (A) But Mike did.　　　　(C) Neither did Mike.
   (B) But Mike didn't.　　　(D) So did Mike.

12. — Andrea speaks fluent French.　　　　　　　　　　　　A B C D

    — _____

   (A) Neither does Paul.　　(C) So is Paul.
   (B) So does Paul.　　　　 (D) So Paul does.

13. — I won't be at Judy's party next week.　　　　　　　　　A B C D
    — Neither _____, and it's too bad. It's going to be a great party.

   (A) I will　　　　　　　(C) am I
   (B) will I　　　　　　　(D) I'll be

14. The hotel _____ expensive, and so were the restaurants.　　A B C D

   (A) was　　　　　　　　(C) were
   (B) wasn't　　　　　　　(D) weren't

PART TWO

Each sentence has four underlined words or phrases. The four underlined parts of the sentence are marked A, B, C, and D. Circle the letter of the <u>one</u> underlined word or phrase that is NOT CORRECT.

Example

Rosa <u>rarely</u> <u>is using</u> public transportation, but <u>today</u> she <u>is taking</u> the bus.
    A   B   C   D
    A Ⓑ C D

15. <u>This</u> <u>isn't</u> the way to Route 101, <u>is</u> <u>this</u>?
    A   B   C D
    A B C D

16. Mary isn't <u>working</u> on Saturday <u>morning</u>, <u>isn't</u> <u>she</u>?
               A   B   C   D
    A B C D

17. Jeff <u>bought</u> a new car, <u>and</u> <u>so</u> <u>does</u> Ann.
       A   B   C D
    A B C D

18. Rachel <u>didn't</u> <u>go</u> to class today, <u>and</u> her sister <u>did</u>.
         A   B   C   D
    A B C D

19. I <u>didn't enjoy</u> the movie, <u>and</u> Frank <u>did</u> <u>either</u>.
     A   B   C   D
    A B C D

20. Vilma <u>is coming</u> to the movies with us, <u>and</u> <u>so</u> <u>Craig is</u>.
         A   B   C   D
    A B C D

Test: Units 9–10

PART ONE

Circle the letter of the correct answer to complete each sentence.

Example

Mark _____ a headache last night.   Ⓐ B C D

(A) had   (C) has had
(B) has   (D) was having

1. _____ the streets safe again is the mayor's highest priority.   A B C D

   (A) Is making   (C) Makes
   (B) Make   (D) Making

2. Geraldo is looking forward to _____ a father.   A B C D

   (A) became   (C) becomes
   (B) becoming   (D) become

3. It was very difficult _____ a good job.   A B C D

   (A) find   (C) has found
   (B) found   (D) to find

4. Elliot bought an exercise video _____ him get into shape.   A B C D

   (A) helped   (C) help
   (B) helps   (D) to help

5. It's time _____ where we want to go this summer.   A B C D

   (A) to decide   (C) deciding
   (B) decides   (D) decide

6. I'm sorry, but I forgot _____ that book you asked for.   A B C D

   (A) bring   (C) to bring
   (B) bringing   (D) brought

7. I can't imagine _____ that.   A B C D

   (A) do   (C) you to do
   (B) to do   (D) your doing

8. Pat invited _____ the weekend with them.   A B C D

   (A) to spend   (C) me to spend
   (B) me spend   (D) my spending

9. The judge made the witness _____ the question.   A   B   C   D

    (A) answer   (C) answering
    (B) answered   (D) to answer

10. Because the restaurant is so popular, I suggest _____ a reservation.   A   B   C   D

    (A) make   (C) makes
    (B) making   (D) to make

11. I studied a lot, so I expected _____ the test.   A   B   C   D

    (A) passed   (C) pass
    (B) passing   (D) to pass

12. Most teachers won't let their students _____ a dictionary during an exam.   A   B   C   D

    (A) use   (C) using
    (B) to use   (D) are using

PART TWO

Each sentence has four underlined words or phrases. The four underlined parts of the sentence are marked A, B, C, and D. Circle the letter of the one underlined word or phrase that is NOT CORRECT.

    Example
    Rosa <u>rarely</u> <u>is using</u> public transportation, but <u>today</u> she <u>is taking</u> the bus.   A Ⓑ C D
        A   B   C   D

13. I <u>got</u> all my friends <u>help</u> <u>me</u> <u>move</u> last June.   A   B   C   D
    A   B C D

14. Phil decided <u>changing</u> jobs because his boss always <u>made</u> <u>him</u> <u>work</u> late.   A   B   C   D
              A   B   C D

15. The students of Maitlin High <u>appreciated</u> their <u>principal's</u> <u>try</u> <u>to improve</u>   A   B   C   D
                                  A   B   C   D

    conditions in their school.

16. Because she wants <u>to be</u> a good boss, Sally can't help <u>to feel</u> responsible for   A   B   C   D
                    A   B

    <u>everyone's</u> <u>doing</u> the work on time.
       C   D

17. Robert <u>succeeded in</u> <u>to find</u> a job after high school, so his parents <u>didn't make</u>   A   B   C   D
             A   B   C

    him <u>apply</u> to college.
       D

18. If you insist <u>on</u> <u>looking</u> over the report, please <u>remember</u> <u>returning</u> it by   A   B   C   D
               A B   C   D

    Monday.

19. <u>Going</u> on a diet doesn't <u>seem</u> <u>to be</u> the best way <u>losing</u> weight.   A   B   C   D
    A   B   C   D

20. Because my husband was <u>planning</u> <u>to go</u> to the post office, I <u>asked him</u> <u>mail</u>   A   B   C   D
                  A   B   C   D

    a package for me.

Test: Units 11–12

PART ONE

Circle the letter of the correct answer to complete each sentence.

Example

Mark _____ a headache last night.　　　　　　　　　　　Ⓐ B C D

(A) had　　　　　　　　　(C) has had
(B) has　　　　　　　　　(D) was having

1. Jan is my best friend. I can always count _____ her.　　A B C D

(A) for　　　　　　　　　(C) on
(B) with　　　　　　　　(D) out

2. Your mother called. She wants you to call her _____ tonight.　A B C D

(A) back　　　　　　　　(C) off
(B) in　　　　　　　　　(D) over

3. That's very original. How did you dream _____ that idea?　A B C D

(A) about　　　　　　　(C) of
(B) down　　　　　　　(D) up

4. — It's cold outside. You need your jacket.　　　　　　　A B C D
   — OK. I'll put _____.

(A) it on　　　　　　　(C) on it
(B) it over　　　　　　(D) over it

5. Some damage was brought _____ by high winds.　　　　A B C D

(A) about　　　　　　　(C) down
(B) across　　　　　　　(D) through

6. Come in. Please sit _____.　　　　　　　　　　　　A B C D

(A) down　　　　　　　(C) it down
(B) down it　　　　　　(D) up

7. Every spring, Marta _____ away some clothes to a local charity.　A B C D

(A) gives　　　　　　　(C) puts
(B) keeps　　　　　　　(D) throws

8. I can hardly hear the TV. Could you turn it _____?　　A B C D

(A) in　　　　　　　　　(C) on
(B) off　　　　　　　　(D) up

9. She ran _____ on the way to the supermarket.   A B C D

    (A) him into   (C) into Jason
    (B) into   (D) Jason into

10. It's too cold to take your gloves off. _____   A B C D

    (A) Keep on.   (C) Keep on them.
    (B) Keep them.   (D) Keep them on.

11. Erika wants to quit, but she says she'll _____.   A B C D

    (A) give up   (C) see through the project
    (B) see the project through (D) see through it

PART TWO

Each sentence has four underlined words or phrases. The four underlined parts of the sentence are marked A, B, C, and D. Circle the letter of the <u>one</u> underlined word or phrase that is NOT CORRECT.

Example
Rosa <u>rarely</u> <u>is using</u> public transportation, but <u>today</u> she <u>is taking</u> the bus.   A Ⓑ C D
    A   B   C   D

12. Could we talk <u>over it</u> before you <u>turn</u> <u>the whole idea</u> <u>down</u>?   A B C D
              A   B   C   D

13. I <u>let</u> <u>Andy</u> <u>down</u> when I forgot to pick his suit <u>out</u> from the cleaner's.   A B C D
   A   B   C   D

14. After Joanne's boss <u>looked</u> <u>over her proposal</u> to redesign the company's   A B C D
                    A   B

    website, he decided to <u>go along</u> <u>her ideas with</u>.
                      C   D

15. After I <u>hand</u> <u>in</u> <u>my report</u>, I'll take all these books <u>on</u> to the library.   A B C D
        A   B   C   D

16. If you can't <u>figure</u> <u>the meaning of a word that you read out</u>, it's a good idea   A B C D
             A   B

    to <u>look</u> <u>it up</u> in a dictionary.
       C   D

17. Even a difficult project will <u>turn out</u> well if you <u>come up</u> <u>to an organized plan</u>   A B C D
                    A   B   C

    and stick <u>to it</u>.
          D

18. Instead of <u>calling</u> <u>off</u> the meeting, let's just <u>put it</u> <u>over</u> until next week.   A B C D
           A   B   C   D

19. If you don't use <u>out</u> the milk by Monday, please <u>throw</u> <u>it</u> <u>away</u>.   A B C D
              A   B C D

20. Greg <u>called up</u> Yuan to <u>cheer up her</u> after her English professor told her to   A B C D
          A   B

    <u>do her research paper</u> <u>over</u>.
         C   D

Test: Units 13–14

PART ONE

*Circle the letter of the correct answer to complete each sentence. Choose (——) when the sentence does not need a relative pronoun or **when**.*

Example

Mark _____ a headache last night.   Ⓐ B C D

(**A**) had   (**C**) has had
(**B**) has   (**D**) was having

1. Our family home, _____ my grandfather built, was on a busy corner.   A B C D

   (**A**) where   (**C**) whose
   (**B**) which   (**D**) that

2. Lisa, _____ I've already mentioned, wrote me a letter.   A B C D

   (**A**) which   (**C**) that
   (**B**) whom   (**D**) ———

3. Those are the people _____ I told you about.   A B C D

   (**A**) where   (**C**) whose
   (**B**) which   (**D**) ———

4. Do you remember the day _____ we found that old bookstore?   A B C D

   (**A**) where   (**C**) whom
   (**B**) whose   (**D**) when

5. Can you hand me the book _____ is on the top shelf?   A B C D

   (**A**) that   (**C**) who
   (**B**) where   (**D**) ———

6. Do you know the man _____ sister works in the library?   A B C D

   (**A**) that   (**C**) who
   (**B**) which   (**D**) whose

7. Mr. Jay, _____ owns the hardware store, comes from my hometown.   A B C D

   (**A**) that   (**C**) whom
   (**B**) who   (**D**) whose

8. Tell me about the city _____ you grew up.

    (A) that   (C) which

    (B) where   (D) ———

A B C D

9. Tony loved the book _____ I lent him.

    (A) when   (C) whose

    (B) who   (D) ———

A B C D

10. The Louvre, _____ is a world-famous museum, is located in Paris.

    (A) that   (C) who

    (B) which   (D) ———

A B C D

11. The candidate for _____ I voted lost the election.

    (A) that   (C) who

    (B) which   (D) whom

A B C D

12. I often think back on the time _____ we traveled together.

    (A) where   (C) who

    (B) which   (D) ———

A B C D

PART TWO

Each sentence has four underlined words or phrases. The four underlined parts of the sentence are marked A, B, C, and D. Circle the letter of the <u>one</u> underlined word or phrase that is NOT CORRECT.

Example

Rosa <u>rarely</u> <u>is using</u> public transportation, but <u>today</u> she <u>is taking</u> the bus.
    A   B   C   D

A Ⓑ C D

13. The woman <u>who</u> <u>she</u> <u>lives</u> next door <u>is</u> very nice.
          A   B   C   D

A B C D

14. One <u>singer</u> <u>who's</u> voice <u>I</u> <u>like</u> is Mary Grant.
     A   B   C D

A B C D

15. The <u>stories</u> <u>what</u> <u>are in this book</u> <u>have</u> wonderful illustrations.
     A   B   C   D

A B C D

16. I <u>enjoyed</u> reading the article <u>that</u> you <u>told</u> me about <u>it</u>.
   A   B   C   D

A B C D

17. I've read some <u>books</u> <u>that</u> <u>discusses</u> the time <u>when</u> this area was undeveloped.
             A   B   C   D

A B C D

18. <u>San Francisco,</u> <u>that</u> <u>is</u> a beautiful <u>city</u>, has a very diverse population.
    A   B C   D

A B C D

19. Do you know the name of the person <u>whom</u> wrote the <u>song</u> <u>that</u> Al
                                 A   B C

    <u>was singing</u> last night?
     D

A B C D

20. That's the man <u>whose</u> sister <u>work</u> in the store <u>that</u> <u>is</u> on Fifth Street.
             A   B   C D

A B C D

Test: Units 15–17

Circle the letter of the correct answer to complete each sentence.

Example

Mark _____ a headache last night.   Ⓐ B C D

(A) had   (C) has had
(B) has   (D) was having

1. We're going to be late. We _____ left earlier.   A B C D

   (A) should   (C) shouldn't
   (B) should have   (D) shouldn't have

2. You _____ Elena. It was a secret.   A B C D

   (A) might not have told   (C) shouldn't have told
   (B) must not have told   (D) couldn't have told

3. — Was it cold last night?   A B C D
   — It _____. The streets were icy this morning.

   (A) could have   (C) had to have been
   (B) had to have   (D) ought to have been

4. You _____ take an umbrella. It isn't going to rain.   A B C D

   (A) don't have to   (C) must
   (B) have to   (D) must not

5. — Are the Martins at home?   A B C D
   — They _____. None of the lights are on.

   (A) could   (C) couldn't
   (B) could be   (D) couldn't be

6. Jack is really unhappy at work. He ought _____ for another job.   A B C D

   (A) have looked   (C) to have looked
   (B) have to look   (D) to look

7. — I'm sorry I'm late.
   — You _____. I've been waiting for an hour.   A B C D

   (A) might not have called   **(C)** might not call
   (B) could have called   **(D)** could not have called

8. — Should he have called the police?   A B C D
   — Yes, he _____.

   (A) did   **(C)** should
   (B) has   **(D)** should have

9. — Did we pay the electric bill last month?   A B C D
   — We _____. We got a late notice today.

   (A) could have   **(C)** must not have
   (B) shouldn't have   **(D)** had to have

10. — I'm sorry I had to cancel our date.   A B C D
    — Oh, I couldn't have _____ anyway. I got sick.

    (A) be going   **(C)** gone
    (B) go   **(D)** went

11. I _____ to finish my research paper last night because I was too tired.   A B C D

    (A) wasn't able   **(C)** couldn't
    (B) weren't able   **(D)** can't

12. — Did the Johnsons see the pyramids on their vacation?   A B C D
    — They _____. Everyone who visits Egypt sees the pyramids.

    (A) could have   **(C)** might have
    (B) may have   **(D)** must have

13. — Are you going to the school dance next weekend?   A B C D
    — I _____ go after I finish work. It'll depend on how tired I am.

    (A) might   **(C)** had better
    (B) must   **(D)** should

14. That's impossible! Janet _____ have known about her surprise party.   A B C D

    (A) couldn't   **(C)** ought not to
    (B) might not   **(D)** shouldn't

PART TWO

Each sentence has four underlined words or phrases. The four underlined parts of the sentence are marked A, B, C, and D. Circle the letter of the <u>one</u> underlined word or phrase that is NOT CORRECT.

Example

Rosa <u>rarely</u> <u>is using</u> public transportation, but <u>today</u> she <u>is taking</u> the bus.
    A   B   C   D

A Ⓑ C D

15. I'm <u>not sure</u>, but Mary <u>could</u> <u>of</u> <u>moved</u>.
        A   B C D

A B C D

16. Fastfoods Restaurant <u>might</u> <u>has</u> <u>gone</u> out of business because the owners
                              A   B   C

A B C D

<u>couldn't</u> keep the prices low.
  D

17. Students <u>must not</u> <u>go</u> to a computer lab at school to do their assignments if
              A   B

A B C D

they <u>can</u> <u>do</u> their work on a computer at home.
     C   D

18. Felicia <u>didn't</u> <u>wave</u> to me, so she <u>must have</u> <u>seen</u> me.
        A   B   C   D

A B C D

19. We <u>ought to have</u> <u>looked at</u> more apartments before we <u>rent</u> this one, but we
        A   B   C

A B C D

<u>had to</u> make a quick decision.
  D

20. Your husband <u>maybe</u> worried, so you <u>should</u> <u>call</u> him to let him know that
               A   B   C

A B C D

you <u>can't</u> get home in time for dinner.
   D

Test: Units 18–20

PART ONE

Circle the letter of the correct answer to complete each sentence.

Example

Mark _____ a headache last night.   Ⓐ B C D

(**A**) had   (**C**) has had
(**B**) has   (**D**) was having

1. That novel was written _____ Anita Shreve.   A B C D

(**A**) at   (**C**) from
(**B**) by   (**D**) to

2. — Do you cut your own hair?   A B C D
   — No. I _____.

(**A**) cut it   (**C**) have it cut
(**B**) have cut it   (**D**) haven't

3. This magazine _____ by many people.   A B C D

(**A**) are read   (**C**) is reading
(**B**) is read   (**D**) reads

4. _____ these books published in Europe?   A B C D

(**A**) Do   (**C**) Was
(**B**) Have   (**D**) Were

5. — When _____ your house built?   A B C D
   — In 1985. It's not a new house.

(**A**) does   (**C**) is
(**B**) has   (**D**) was

6. Bill Gates _____ millions of dollars to charity.   A B C D

(**A**) is given   (**C**) was given
(**B**) has given   (**D**) had been given

7. The report _____ soon.   A B C D

(**A**) will have published   (**C**) will be published
(**B**) will be publishing   (**D**) will publish

(continued)

8. — When can we see the finished product?
    — The work _____ before the end of the year, but I'm not really sure.

    (A) might have completed   (C) may complete
    (B) might be completed   (D) must complete

A   B   C   D

9. How many times have you had to get your car _____ since you bought it?

    (A) fix   (C) been fixed
    (B) fixed   (D) to fix

A   B   C   D

10. I think she usually _____ her own clothes.

    (A) have made   (C) is made
    (B) has them made   (D) makes

A   B   C   D

PART TWO

Each sentence has four underlined words or phrases. The four underlined parts of the sentence are marked A, B, C, and D. Circle the letter of the <u>one</u> underlined word or phrase that is NOT CORRECT.

Example
Rosa <u>rarely is using</u> public transportation, but <u>today</u> she <u>is taking</u> the bus.
   A   B   C   D

A   Ⓑ   C   D

11. That movie <u>was</u> <u>filmed</u> <u>from</u> <u>an award-winning director</u>.
             A   B   C   D

A   B   C   D

12. Before a final decision <u>is reached</u>, the various possibilities <u>should</u> probably
                        A   B

    <u>discussed</u> <u>by</u> the whole team.
      C   D

A   B   C   D

13. I <u>can</u> <u>do</u> my own taxes, but I usually <u>have done them</u> <u>by</u> an accountant.
    A   B   C   D

A   B   C   D

14. The house <u>painted</u> three years ago, but I'm not <u>planning</u> to <u>have</u> <u>it done</u>
              A   B   C   D

    again for a while.

A   B   C   D

15. According to some experts, the amount of homework that students <u>are</u> <u>given</u>
                                                                A   B

    must <u>be limited</u>, but I <u>am not</u> agree.
         C   D

A   B   C   D

16. A lot of crops <u>can't</u> be <u>grown</u> <u>by people</u> because the weather <u>gets</u> too cold
                    A   B   C   D

    in the mountains.

A   B   C   D

17. That dinosaur <u>was</u> <u>find</u> <u>by Sue Hendrickson</u> while she <u>was working</u> in the
                   A   B   C   D

    Black Hills of South Dakota.

A   B   C   D

18. When we <u>visit</u> Machu Picchu, we <u>should</u> <u>have</u> our pictures <u>took</u> in front of   **A B C D**
            A   **B**   **C**   **D**
     the famous Inca ruins.

19. You <u>had better</u> <u>be get</u> the locks <u>changed</u> after you <u>move</u> into your new   **A B C D**
           A   **B**   **C**   **D**
     apartment.

20. When the *Titanic* <u>was</u> <u>launched</u> in 1912, it <u>was carried</u> 1,316 passengers   **A B C D**
                    A   **B**   **C**
     who <u>were traveling</u> from England to the United States.
           D

Test: Units 21–24

PART ONE

Circle the letter of the correct answer to complete each sentence.

Example

Mark _____ a headache last night.   Ⓐ B C D

(A) had   (C) has had
(B) has   (D) was having

1. If you _____ any questions, ask.   A B C D

   (A) had had   (C) have
   (B) had   (D) will have

2. If you heat air, it _____.   A B C D

   (A) is rising   (C) rises
   (B) rise   (D) rose

3. If I understood Professor Patel's lecture, I _____ it to you.   A B C D

   (A) could explain   (C) could have explained
   (B) can explain   (D) may explain

4. I'd call her if I _____ her number.   A B C D

   (A) know   (C) would know
   (B) knew   (D) will know

5. What will you do if the letter _____ arrive by tomorrow?   A B C D

   (A) doesn't   (C) won't
   (B) didn't   (D) wouldn't

6. _____ you have a license, you can't drive in California.   A B C D

   (A) Because   (C) Unless
   (B) If   (D) When

7. If I _____ you, I'd call the doctor.   A B C D

   (A) am   (C) were
   (B) was   (D) would be

8. What would you do if you _____ the lottery?   A B C D

   (A) 're winning   (C) won
   (B) win   (D) would win

9. I wish you _____ me an e-mail sometime soon. A B C D

    (A) would have sent   (C) sent
    (B) had sent   (D) would send

10. — If you knew the answer, would you tell me? A B C D
    — Yes, I _____.

    (A) did   (C) would
    (B) will   (D) would have

11. Where _____ you go if you wanted to rent a car? A B C D

    (A) can   (C) would
    (B) do   (D) will

12. Now Don wishes he _____ studying English years ago. A B C D

    (A) had started   (C) starts
    (B) is starting   (D) started

13. If you _____ us about the movie, we wouldn't have gone to see it. A B C D

    (A) didn't tell   (C) hadn't told
    (B) wouldn't have told   (D) haven't told

14. The team _____ their last game if the coach had let Tyler play. A B C D

    (A) could win   (C) might have won
    (B) had to win   (D) might win

PART TWO

Each sentence has four underlined words or phrases. The four underlined parts of the sentence are marked A, B, C, and D. Circle the letter of the <u>one</u> underlined word or phrase that is NOT CORRECT.

    Example
    Rosa <u>rarely</u> <u>is using</u> public transportation, but <u>today</u> she <u>is taking</u> the bus. A Ⓑ C D
       A   B   C   D

15. <u>If</u> Joan <u>had been</u> there yesterday, you <u>would have</u> <u>see</u> her. A B C D
   A   B   C   D

16. My mother <u>wishes</u> she <u>went</u> to medical school <u>when</u> she <u>was</u> younger. A B C D
        A   B   C   D

17. I <u>would</u> <u>tell</u> her the truth <u>if</u> I <u>am</u> you. A B C D
   A   B   C D

18. We <u>wish</u> that our parents <u>could read</u> us bedtime stories <u>when</u> we <u>were</u> little. A B C D
     A   B   C   D

19. Our plans won't <u>work</u> <u>unless</u> we all don't <u>try</u> <u>harder</u>. A B C D
        A   B   C   D

20. <u>If</u> you hadn't <u>driven</u> me to the station, I <u>might not</u> <u>of</u> caught the train. A B C D
   A   B   C   D

Test: Units 25–29

PART ONE

Circle the letter of the correct answer to complete each sentence.

Example

Mark _____ a headache last night.   Ⓐ B C D

(A) had   (C) has had
(B) has   (D) was having

1. — Does Pedro live around here?   A B C D
   — I'm not sure _____ in this neighborhood.

   (A) does he live   (C) if he lives
   (B) if does he live   (D) if or not he lives

2. "When can you finish the marketing report?"   A B C D
   Last week my boss asked me _____ the marketing report.

   (A) when can I finish   (C) when I could finish
   (B) that when I can finish (D) when could I finish

3. Ann's friends all asked her why _____ that job.   A B C D

   (A) did she accept   (C) she had accepted
   (B) did you accept   (D) she accepts

4. — Do you know what _____?   A B C D
   — No. I'm sorry, but I don't.

   (A) is that man's name   (C) 's that man's name
   (B) that man's name   (D) that man's name is

5. "I handed in my paper yesterday."   A B C D
   Last Wednesday, Shuwen said that he had handed in his paper _____.

   (A) that day   (C) the next day
   (B) yesterday   (D) the day before

6. "We've never eaten sushi."   A B C D
   Before they went to Japan, the Smiths said that they _____ sushi.

   (A) never eat   (C) 'd never eaten
   (B) 've never eaten   (D) 'd never have eaten

7. He _____, "The rent is due on the first of the month."　　　　A　B　C　D

    (A) asked　　　　　　　(C) told
    (B) said　　　　　　　　(D) wanted to know

8. **Expert to reporter:** "Weather patterns change. We all agree about that."　　A　B　C　D
   Newspaper story: Experts say that weather patterns _____.

    (A) change　　　　　　(C) were changing
    (B) changed　　　　　　(D) had changed

9. — I read your report.　　　　　　　　　　　　　　　　　　A　B　C　D
   — Oh. What did you think of it?
   Al told Barbara that he had read _____ report.

    (A) her　　　　　　　　(C) my
    (B) his　　　　　　　　(D) your

10. Ten years ago, Tanya told John that she _____ marry him.　　A　B　C　D

    (A) isn't going to　　　(C) won't
    (B) can't　　　　　　　(D) wouldn't

11. The police officer told us _____.　　　　　　　　　　　A　B　C　D

    (A) stop　　　　　　　(C) that to stop
    (B) stopped　　　　　　(D) to stop

12. She asked us _____ so loud because she was trying to study.　　A　B　C　D

    (A) don't talk　　　　　(C) talk
    (B) not to talk　　　　　(D) to talk

PART TWO

Each sentence has four underlined words or phrases. The four underlined parts of the sentence are marked A, B, C, and D. Circle the letter of the one underlined word or phrase that is NOT CORRECT.

Example
Rosa <u>rarely is using</u> public transportation, but <u>today</u> she <u>is taking</u> the bus.　　A　Ⓑ　C　D
    A　　　B　　　　　　　　　　　　　　C　　　　D

13. The teacher <u>said</u> her students <u>that</u> she <u>was going to</u> give <u>them</u> an important　　A　B　C　D
        A　　　　　　　　　　B　　　　C　　　　　　D

   research assignment.

14. At 9:00 P.M. last Friday, my boss <u>called</u> me and <u>told</u> me I <u>have to</u> go into the　　A　B　C　D
                    A　　　　　　B　　　　C

   office <u>the next day</u>.
       D

(continued)

15. I'll never forget August 13, 2004, because I <u>heard</u> on the radio <u>that</u> a

                                                 A   **B**

    hurricane <u>is coming</u> <u>that afternoon</u>.

                    C   **D**

                  A B C D

16. Gloria e-mailed me last week and <u>wanted to know</u> <u>if</u> I <u>could</u> give her the

                                      A   **B**   **C**

    information that she needed right <u>now</u>.

                                  D

                  A B C D

17. We <u>invited</u> <u>her</u> <u>visit</u> our class <u>last semester</u>.

           A   **B** **C**   **D**

                  A B C D

18. Bob <u>asked</u> <u>me</u> <u>that</u> I <u>wanted</u> to go to a movie.

         A   **B** **C**   **D**

                  A B C D

19. The new secretary <u>asked</u> me <u>how</u> I <u>pronounced</u> my name<u>?</u>

                    A   **B**   **C**   **D**

                  A B C D

20. <u>Could</u> you <u>tell</u> me <u>what time</u> <u>is it</u>?

     A   **B**   **C**   **D**

                  A B C D

Answer Key for Tests

Correct responses for Part Two questions appear in parentheses.

UNITS 1–4

Part One

1. A
2. C
3. B
4. C
5. D
6. C
7. B
8. D
9. A
10. B
11. D
12. A

Part Two

13. D (were sleeping)
14. C (gave)
15. C ('m waiting)
16. B (got)
17. D (saw)
18. D (graduated)
19. B (hadn't)
20. A (have)

UNITS 5–6

Part One

1. B
2. B
3. B
4. A
5. D
6. C
7. A
8. D
9. C
10. A

Part Two

11. B (be)
12. B (washes)
13. B (get)
14. C ('ll call OR 's going to call OR 'll be calling)
15. A (will have been saving OR will have saved)
16. A (have)
17. C (working)
18. D (paid)
19. D (pays off)
20. D (carried)

UNITS 7–8

Part One

1. A
2. C
3. A
4. B
5. C
6. A
7. B
8. C
9. B
10. A
11. B
12. B
13. B
14. A

Part Two

15. D (it)
16. C (is)
17. D (did)
18. C (but)
19. C (didn't)
20. D (is Craig)

UNITS 9–10

Part One

1. D
2. B
3. D
4. D
5. A
6. C
7. D
8. C
9. A
10. B
11. D
12. A

Part Two

13. B (to help)
14. A (to change)
15. C (trying)
16. B (feeling)
17. B (finding)
18. D (to return)
19. D (of losing OR to lose)
20. D (to mail)

UNITS 11–12

Part One

1. C
2. A
3. D
4. A
5. A
6. A
7. A
8. D
9. C
10. D
11. B

Part Two

12. A (it over)
13. D (up)
14. D (with her ideas)
15. D (back OR over)

16. B (out the meaning of a word that you read)
17. C (with an organized plan)

18. D (off)
19. A (up)
20. B (cheer her up)

UNITS 13–14

Part One
1. B
2. B
3. D
4. D
5. A
6. D
7. B
8. B
9. D
10. B
11. D
12. D

Part Two
13. B (*delete* she)
14. B (whose)
15. B (that OR which)
16. D (*delete* it)
17. C (discuss)
18. B (which)
19. A (who OR that)
20. B (works)

UNITS 15–17

Part One
1. B
2. C
3. C
4. A
5. D
6. D
7. B
8. D
9. C
10. C
11. A
12. D
13. A
14. A

Part Two
15. C (have)
16. B (have)
17. A (don't have to)
18. C (must not have OR couldn't have)
19. C (rented)
20. A (may be)

UNITS 18–20

Part One
1. B
2. C
3. B
4. D
5. D
6. B
7. C
8. B
9. B
10. D

Part Two
11. C (by)
12. C (be discussed)

13. C (have them done)
14. A (was painted)
15. D (don't OR do not)
16. C (*delete* by people)
17. B (found)
18. D (taken)
19. B (get OR have)
20. C (was carrying OR carried)

UNITS 21–24

Part One
1. C
2. C
3. A
4. B
5. A
6. C
7. C
8. C
9. D
10. C
11. C
12. A
13. C
14. C

Part Two
15. D (seen)
16. B (had gone)
17. D (were)
18. B (could have read OR had read)
19. B (if)
20. D (have)

UNITS 25–29

Part One
1. C
2. C
3. C
4. D
5. D
6. C
7. B
8. A
9. A
10. D
11. D
12. B

Part Two
13. A (told OR said to)
14. C (had to)
15. C (was coming)
16. D (then)
17. C (to visit)
18. C (if OR whether OR whether or not)
19. D (.)
20. D (it is)

Notes

Notes

Notes

Notes